W0008789

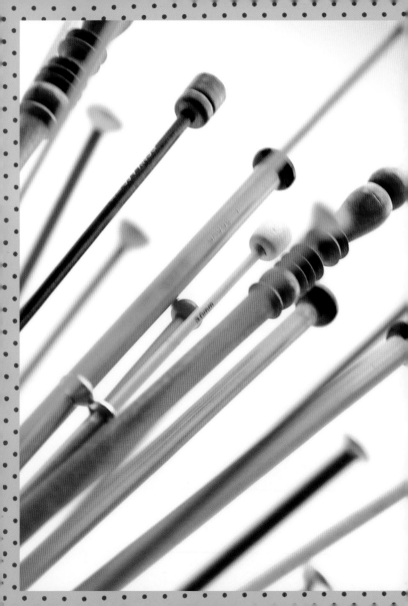

Contents

How To Knit: Basics

Introduction	2
Yarns & Needles	4
Knitting Patterns	10
Casting On & Binding Off	16
Knit & Purl	21
Increasing & Decreasing	23
Special Techniques	27
Decorative Techniques	33
Finishing Techniques	35
Troubleshooting	38
Index	41

Introduction

This book will provide you with all the knitting know-how you'll need to become a confident knitter with essential start-to-finish support from selecting the best yarns and choosing the correct needles, to those all important finishing touches for your knitting projects.

Learn all the basic techniques you will need such as casting on, knit and purl stitches, and binding off. Unlock the hidden code of knitting with the handy guide to reading a pattern with its crystal clear explanation of pattern abbreviations. Be encouraged to try new techniques including the twists and turns of cable panels and colour knitting with intarsia, and bring some extra sparkle to your projects with embellishing techniques such as knitting with beads.

With its easy-to-follow illustrations, helpful tints, and troubleshooting guide, this is an indispensable little book of knitting reference that should always be by your side.

Yarns & Needles

This section tells you everything you need to know when selecting yarns and needles for your knitted projects.

Fibres

One of the joys of being a knitter is being able to explore the fabulous range of yarns available today. Here is an introduction to the many choices that you may be offered when you enter a yarn store.

Natural fibres

Natural fibres can be made from either animal or plant sources. They often feel better than synthetic fibres and take dyes extremely well, so they can offer a greater range of colours. However, they can need careful handling and often need to be washed with care, so you may prefer to choose synthetic fibres for items that have to stand up to heavy wear and frequent cleaning in the washing machine. Natural fibres are often more expensive than synthetic fibres, but they do add a touch of luxury and quality to any item.

Alpaca Spun from the coat of the alpaca to produce a soft and lustrous yarn that has many of the qualities of cashmere but comes at a more affordable price.

Angora Fur of the Angora rabbit is soft and silky and yields a fibre that is fine with a fluffy 'halo'. Items made from angora are beautifully soft and warm and will last for many years if looked after carefully.

Cashmere Plucked from the downy undercoat of the Cashmere goat. The ultimate luxury yarn, it is lightweight, incredibly soft and very warm. It is usually blended with other fibres, such as wool, to produce a soft yarn at a more reasonable price.

Cotton Produced from part of the seed case of the cotton bush. It is a heavy fibre, very hard-wearing and available in a wide range of colours. Cotton can be mercerized to give it lustre and enables it to take brighter dyes. Matte cotton tends to be more loosely spun and is softer.

Linen Part of the stem of the flax plant. It is processed several times to produce a finished fibre that is stiff and crunchy with little elasticity. It is often blended with cotton to soften it, but on its own it has a better drape than cotton.

Mohair This fur comes from the Angora goat and kid mohair comes from young goats of up to 18 months old. The long hairs make a yarn than can be brushed or unbrushed and that is light and airy. Although mohair may be knitted up on its own, it is often blended with other wools and fibres to give it strength.

Silk A continuous filament secreted by the silkworm lava, which it spins around itself to form a cocoon. This cocoon is unwound and many of these fibres are spun together to form a fine, strong yarn. Silk has a wonderful lustre and is soft with a dry feel.

Wool Yarn spun from the fleece of a sheep. Different breeds of sheep produce different types of wool. Lambswool is the first shearing from an animal and is softer than subsequent shearings. Wool is a versatile yarn, being warm in winter and cool in summer. It knits up very well and stands up to unravelling and recycling with no loss of quality.

Blended and synthetic fibres

Man-made yarns use substances that are not fibres originally but are made into fibres by the addition of chemicals. Synthetic yarns are durable and can be machine washed. They are often added to natural fibres to make a yarn that is cheaper and more elastic. Novelty yarns are often made from synthetic fibres. The most commonly used synthetic fibres are polyester, acrylic and polypropylene. Synthetic fibres also take dye well.

Weight

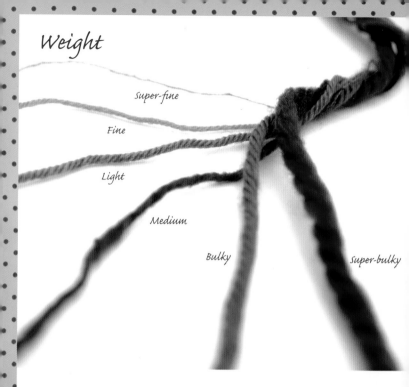

Super-fine

Fine

Light

Medium

Bulky

Super-bulky

The weight of a yarn is its thickness, and this is how yarns are classified. Pattern stitches can look very different when they are knitted in different weights of yarn; a thin, lightweight yarn will produce a soft and delicate fabric, whereas a thick, medium weight yarn will produce a thick, heavy fabric. Why not experiment for yourself with different yarn weights to see the effects that you can get?

TIP
When learning to knit, use a 100 per cent wool yarn; it can be unravelled and reused if needs be.

Ply or thickness

A strand of spun yarn is called a single and plied yarn is created from singles twisted together, usually two, three or four plies. However, while the general rule is that the more plies twisted together, the thicker the yarn will be, this is not always the case because a ply could be large or small depending on the original fibre. The thickness of the yarn is also affected by the spinning process; a tightly spun ply will be thinner than a loosely spun ply.

TIP
Always use scissors to cut yarn. Never be tempted to break it as you will stretch the fibres.

To add to the confusion, yarn manufacturers in the US and UK sometimes use different names for the same weight of yarn. Therefore the yarn requirements described in this book follow the standard developed by the Craft Yarn Council of America, which divides yarns into weights rather than numbers of plies, with the common UK equivalent given in brackets. Using the chart below, you should be able to find a suitable yarn for any of the projects in this book no matter where in the world you buy your yarn.

STANDARD YARN WEIGHTS

weight	gauge*	needle size**	yarn type***
super-fine	27–32 sts	1 to 3 (2.25–3.25mm)	sock, fingering (2ply, 3ply)
fine	23–26 sts	3 to 5 (3.25–3.75mm)	sport, baby (4ply)
light	21–24 sts	5 to 7 (3.75–4.5mm)	light worsted, DK (DK)
medium	16–20 sts	7 to 9 (4.5–5.5mm)	worsted, afghan (aran)
bulky	12–15 sts	9 to 11 (5.5–8mm)	chunky
super-bulky	6–11 sts	11 (8mm) and above	super-chunky

Notes: * Gauge (tension) is measured over 4in/10cm in stockinette (stocking) stitch
** US needle sizes are given first, with UK equivalents in brackets
*** Alternative US yarn type names are given first, with UK equivalents in brackets

Colour & Texture

One of the most exciting things about knitting is the chance to experiment with colour and texture. Yarns come in many forms all of which have their own special characteristics.

1 Self-striping yarn has long lengths of colour that slowly merge into the next colour. To heighten the effect, use two balls of yarn as you work, knitting two rows with one and two rows with the other.

2 Ribbon yarn is a woven tape that produces a flat yarn. and it is available in many different fibres.

3 Short-pile eyelash yarn resembles frayed ribbon. It can have short splashes of colour that merge through the texture of the yarn.

4 Tweed yarn is a marl of two or more colours punctuated with flecks of contrasting colours.

5 Long-pile eyelash yarn knits up into a fabric of deep, shimmering waves with randomly placed colours.

6 Striped yarn is designed for smaller projects. In the example opposite each colour is separated by a dark blue stripe, so they are all clearly defined and do not merge with each other. Try using two balls at once, as with self-striping yarn, to break the sequence, or use two strands together to produce a marl yarn.

Needles

There are three different types of needle:

Straight needles Used in pairs and have a point at one end and a fixed knob at the other. Stitches are worked using the pointed end; they cannot be removed from the other end. They are used for flat knitting, working across a row of stitches moving from one needle to the other; turning the work and working back again, and continuing back and forth.

Double-pointed needles These are used in sets of four or five and have a point at each end. Stitches can be worked with one end and can also be removed from the other end. This means that you don't have to turn your work at the end of each row. In fact you can continue knitting in a spiral and produce a seamless continuous tube. This is called circular knitting.

Circular needles These consist of a pair of needles joined by a flexible nylon wire. They have a point at each end and, like double-pointed needles, you can work from both end and so knit in rounds to produce a seamless tube.

Needle lengths

There are three standard lengths: 10in (25cm), 12in (30cm) and 14in (35cm). Use the length appropriate to the number of stitches: stitches should fit snugly along the length of the needle, not crammed together where they can easily fall off the end.

> **TIP**
> Invest in a needle gauge to check the size of a needle: circular and double-pointed needles tend not to be marked.

NEEDLE SIZES

US	Metric	US	Metric
0	2mm	10	6mm
1	2.25mm	10½	6.5mm
	2.5mm		7mm
2	2.75mm		7.5mm
	3mm	11	8mm
3	3.25mm	13	9mm
4	3.5mm	15	10mm
5	3.75mm	17	12.75mm
6	4mm	19	15mm
7	4.5mm	35	19mm
8	5mm		20mm
9	5.5mm		

CROCHET HOOKS

US	Metric	US	Metric
B1	2.5mm	19	5.5mm
C2	2.75mm	J10	6mm
D3	3.25mm	K10½	6.5mm
E4	3.5mm	L11	8mm
F5	3.75mm	M/N13	9mm
G6	4mm	N/P15	10mm
7	4.5mm	P/Q	15mm
H8	5mm		

Knitting Patterns

A knitting pattern provides you with all the instructions you need to make a project. It will tell you the type of yarn you will need, the size of needles, the gauge you need to achieve as you knit, and provide you with the instructions to make the project you have chosen.

Gauge

Gauge (tension) is the resistance on the yarn as it passes through your fingers as you knit. Keeping a moderate, consistent and correct tension will produce an even fabric. All patterns will specify the gauge that needs to be achieved to knit the project to the correct size. It is stated as the number of stitches and rows you need to make 4in (10cm) of fabric. It is important to take time to achieve the correct gauge if you want your project to be the same size as on the pattern.

Gauge measurement

To check your gauge, work a square of fabric that measures at least 6in (15cm) using the stated yarn, needle size and stitch. This allows you to measure the fabric in the middle of the square, away from the edges, which may be distorted. You will not always be able to achieve both the correct stitch and row count. In these circumstances,

it is more important to achieve the correct stitch count, as otherwise the item will be either too wide or not wide enough. Row count is less important as you can knit fewer or more rows to achieve the desired length if necessary. Row count becomes important when decrease instructions are given over an exact number of rows. If your row tension is not accurate, you may have to recalculate these decreases to ensure the item is the right length.

Knitting a gauge square

Knit a gauge square in stockinette (stocking) stitch by casting on the number of stitches stated to measure 4in (10cm) plus half as many again.

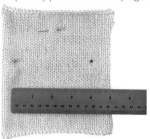

1 Work in stockinette stitch for 6in (15cm) and bind off loosely.

2 Block the square in the same way that you will the finished item (see page 35).

3 Lay your square out on a flat surface without stretching it. Using a ruler, measure and mark with a pin 1in (2.5cm) in from one edge, and then 4in (10cm) from that pin.

4 For the rows, place the ruler vertically on the square and mark the same measurements, avoiding the cast-on and bound-off edges, which may pull the fabric in.

5 Count the number of stitches and rows between the pins to get your gauge. If you have more stitches than the pattern states, your stitches are too small; try knitting the gauge square again with a size larger needle. If you have fewer stitches than the pattern states, your stitches are to big; try knitting the gauge square again with a size smaller needle.

6 Continue to adjust needle sizes and knit gauge squares until you achieve the gauge stated in the pattern.

Measuring textured yarn

Yarn that has a lot of texture or long pile can be difficult to measure. Mark the measurements on long-pile yarns with long pieces of yarn in a contrasting colour. To make the stitches easier to see, try holding the fabric up to a window or a light. Take care to protect your eyes from strong light.

For textured yarn such as bouclé or chenille, knit sewing cotton in a contrasting colour in with the yarn as you make your square. This helps to show up the stitches. Again, mark the measurements with pieces of yarn in a contrasting colour instead of pins. This allows you to pull the fabric slightly to identify difficult stitches without the pins falling out.

If you are still having difficulty, try counting the stitches on the reverse side of the fabric – for stockinette stitch it is often easier to see the stitches on this side when using textured yarn.

Measuring over a stitch pattern

Where the gauge is given over a stitch pattern other than stockinette stitch, cast on enough stitches to work complete repeats of the pattern. The repeat of the pattern is stated after the asterisk, so cast on a multiple of this number of stitches plus any stitches worked at the beginning and end of a row.

Abbreviations

Abbreviations are used in knitting patterns to shorten commonly used terms so that the instructions are easier to read and a manageable length. The following is a list of all the abbreviations you need to make the projects featured in your *How to Knit* box set and many of these are further explained later in this book. The green tinted box opposite lists the most common differences in US and UK knitting terms.

alt	alternate
approx	approximately
beg	beginning
C4B	cable 4 back
C4F	cable 4 front
Cr3L	cross 3 left
Cr3R	cross 3 right
cm	centimetre(s)
cont	continue
dec(s)	decrease/decreasing
DK	double knitting
dpn	double-pointed needles
foll	following
g	gram(s)
g st	garter stitch (k every row)
inc	increase(s)/increasing
in(s)	inch(es)
k	knit
k2tog	knit 2 stitches together (1 stitch decreased)
k3tog	knit 3 stitches together (2 stitches decreased)
k2togtbl	knit 2 stitches together through back of loops (1 stitch decreased)
kf&b	knit into front and back of stitch (increase 1 stitch)
m	metre(s)
mm	millimetres
M1	make one (increase 1 stitch)
oz	ounces
p	purl

US TERM	UK TERM
stockinette stitch	stocking stitch
reverse stockinette stitch	reverse stocking stitch
seed stitch	moss stitch
moss stitch	double moss stitch
bind off	cast off
gauge	tension

patt(s)	pattern(s)
PB	place bead
p2tog	purl 2 stitches together (1 stitch decreased)
p3tog	purl 3 stitches together (2 stitches decreased)
rem	remain/ing
rep(s)	repeat(s)
RS	right side
sk2po	slip 1 stitch, knit 2 stitches together, pass slipped stitch over (decrease 2 stitches)
sl	slip
sl2tog-k1-psso	slip 2 stitches together, knit 1 stitch, pass 2 slipped stitches over (2 stitches decreased)
ssk	slip 2 stitches one at a time, knit 2 slipped stitches together (1 stitch decreased)
st st	stockinette (stocking) stitch
st(s)	stitch(es)
tbl	through back of loop
tog	together
WS	wrong side
wyib	with yarn in back
wyif	with yarn in front
yd(s)	yards(s)
yo	yarn over
*	repeat directions following * as many times as indicated or end of row
[ ]	instructions in square brackets refer to larger sizes
( )	repeat instructions in round brackets the number of times

Reading a Pattern

For reasons of space, patterns use abbreviations and shorthand phrases. The abbreviations used in the patterns in this book are listed on the previous pages. Many abbreviations, such as k and p, are used widely throughout all patterns. Other patterns may have specific abbreviations relating to specific stitches; these should always be explained in full at the beginning of the pattern.

Imperial and metric measurements

The patterns give both imperial measurements (inches and ounces) and metric measurements (centimetres and grams). Make sure you stick to one set of measurements throughout your project; although most conversions are exact, there are some that are more generalized.

COMMON SHORTHAND PHRASES

Cont as set This is used to avoid repeating the same instructions over and over again. Just continue to work as previously instructed. For example: **Row 1** K, **Row 2** P. Cont in st st as set.

Keeping patt correct Again, to avoid repeating instructions, this tells you to ensure you work the pattern as previously instructed, even though you have been told to do something that would otherwise interfere with the pattern. For example: Keeping centre panel pattern correct, cont in st st.

Work as given for This is where you are making two similar items. Instead of repeating the instructions in full as given for the first item,

you are instructed to work the second item in the same way as the first item to a given point, which is usually marked by asterisks.

Reversing all shaping Shaping is given for one piece and the other piece must be shaped to be a mirror image of it.

* Repeat instructions following an asterisk as many times as indicated or until you reach the end of a row.
** Double asterisks usually appear at the beginning and/or end of a section of instructions which will need to be repeated.
( ) Instructions in round brackets should be repeated the indicated number of times.

Sizes

Knitting patterns can be written in more than one size with the smallest size first (outside the brackets) and the remaining sizes inside square brackets, separated by colons. The largest size will be given at the end. Your size will always appear in the same place in the bracket; instructions for the first size will always be first, for the second size they will be second, etc. Square brackets are used to indicate the number of stitches and rows to be worked, or how many times a pattern is repeated for each size. For example, cast on 90 [92: 94: 96] sts, or work patt 1 [2: 3: 4] times. If a zero appears for your size, do not work the instructions it is referring to, for example, dec 3 [0: 1: 2] sts. If only one figure appears then it refers to all sizes.

When stopping knitting make sure you mark in the pattern where you have got to.

Working from charts

Charts for colourwork techniques

Patterns involving the intarsia or Fair Isle colourwork techniques are worked from charts. The pattern will usually give few other instructions, except to tell you how many stitches to cast on and instructions for any parts of the project not included in the chart. See page 32 for how to work from an intarsia chart.

When working from a multi-sized pattern, highlight your size.

Stitch charts

A knitting pattern may contain a stitch chart – an illustration of a cable or lace pattern or a texture pattern with each stitch being represented by a symbol, which usually reflects the texture of a stitch. A knit stitch often appears as a blank square, whilst a purl stitch is a dot or horizontal dash. The key provided alongside a stitch chart will tell you what each symbol means. Many of the stitches described in the *Stitches* book have stitch charts as well as pattern instructions.

Casting On & Binding Off

These are the two key techniques you will need, casting on to get the yarn on to your needle ready to begin work, and binding off, removing the completed project from your needles without it unravelling.

Casting On

To begin knitting, you need to work a foundation row of stitches and this is called casting on. There are several different ways to cast on stitches but some methods are better than others if you want to achieve certain results, so if a particular method is specified in the pattern use it. Otherwise it is purely a matter of personal preference.

Thumb method

This method uses only one needle and is the simplest way of casting on. Unwind a length of yarn from the ball that is enough for the number of stitches you are casting on. Allow approximately 1–1⅛ in (2.5–3cm) per stitch. Make a slip knot at this point on one needle (see The Slip Knot box opposite).

1 Hold the needle with the slip knot in your right hand. Put the ball end of the yarn over the index finger, under the middle finger and over the third finger of your right hand. Wrap the free end of the yarn around the thumb of your left hand from the back.

2 Insert the needle through the thumb loop from front to back.

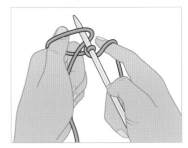

3 Using the index finger of your right hand, wrap the yarn from the ball around the needle.

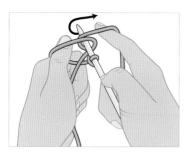

4 Pull the loop on the needle through the loop on your thumb. Slip the loop off your thumb and gently tighten the stitch up to the needle by pulling on both strands of yarn. Repeat until you have cast on the required number of stitches.

TIP

If your casting on is always too tight, use a size larger needle. If it always too loose, use a smaller needle. But always change back to the correct size needle to begin knitting.

THE SLIP KNOT
Follow these simple diagrams to make a slip knot, the first cast on stitch when working the thumb method cast-on. Pull the ends of the yarn to tighten it and you are ready to follow the instructions for casting on.

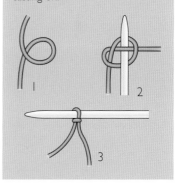

Cable cast-on method

This gives a neat, firm edge that is also elastic making it perfect as an edging for rib stitch. It is also the method used to cast on stitches in the middle of a row. Take two needles; make a slip knot about 6in (15cm) from the end of the yarn on one needle.

1 Insert the right-hand needle knitwise into the loop on the left-hand needle and wrap the yarn around the tip.

2 Pull the yarn through the loop to make a stitch but do not drop the stitch off the left-hand needle.

3 Slip the new stitch onto the left-hand needle by inserting the left-hand needle into the front of the loop from right to left. You will now have two stitches on the left-hand needle.

4 Insert the right-hand needle between the two stitches on the left-hand needle and wrap the yarn around the tip. Pull the yarn back through between the two stitches and place it on the left-hand needle, as in step 3. Repeat until you have cast on the required number of stitches.

To cast on extra stitches mid row
Work step 4 only, working the first stitch between the next two stitches already on the left-hand needle.

Knitting-on method

This produces a fairly loose cast-on row and two needles are used. Using the cable cast-on method, cast on two stitches following steps 1–3. Continue for as many stitches as are needed.

Binding Off

Binding off (casting off) links stitches together so that they cannot unravel and secures stitches when a piece of knitting is complete. Binding off is normally done following the stitch sequence, so a knit stitch is bound off knitwise and a purl stitch purlwise. It is important not to bind off too tightly as this may pull the fabric in.

Bind off knitwise

1 Knit the first two stitches. Insert the point of the left-hand needle into the front of the first stitch on the right-hand needle.

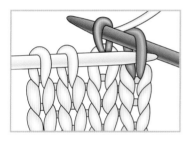

2 Lift the first stitch on the right-hand needle over the second stitch and off the needle.

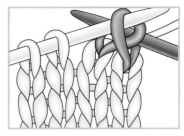

3 One stitch is left on the right-hand needle.

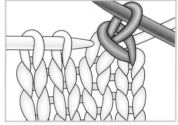

4 Knit the next stitch on the left-hand needle, so there are again two stitches on the right-hand needle. Lift the first stitch on the right-hand needle over the second stitch, as in step 2. Repeat this process until one stitch is left on the right-hand needle. Cut the yarn (leaving a length long enough to sew or weave in) and pass the end through the last stitch. Slip the stitch off the needle and pull the yarn end to tighten it.

TIP
You will often need to leave your work without binding off. Always complete a row – finishing in the middle of a row can cause your stitches to stretch or come off the needle.

Bind off purlwise

To bind off a purl row, all you have to do is purl the stitches instead of knitting them.

Bind off in pattern

When you are knitting in patterns such as rib or cables, it is important to bind off in pattern to maintain an elastic edge. In this case, all that you have to do is knit the knit stitches and purl the purl stitches.

> **TIP**
>
> *Binding off too tightly can cause your fabric to pucker. This is a particular problem on a visible edge, such as on a throw. Try using a needle a size larger than that used to knit the main fabric.*

PICKING UP STITCHES

One piece of knitting can be joined to another by picking up stitches. This eliminates a seam and makes a smoother join. Hold the work in your left hand with the right side facing. With a needle and the yarn in your right hand, insert the needle under the top of the loop of the first stitch. Wrap the yarn knitwise around the needle and draw through a loop. Continue in this way, inserting the needle under the top loop of each stitch until you have the correct number of stitches.

Knit & Purl

(For Continental methods see pp. 42–43)

The two classic knitting stitches are the knit stitch and the purl stitch. Once you know both the knit and purl stitches, you can pretty much make anything.

Knit Stitch

This is the simplest stitch of all and is the one that most people learn first. Each stitch is created with a four-step process. Hold the yarn at the back of the work – this is the side facing away from you.

1 Place the needle with the cast-on stitches in your left hand, insert the right-hand needle into the front of the first stitch on the left-hand needle from left to right.

2 Take the yarn around and under the point of the right-hand needle.

3 Draw the new loop on the right-hand needle through the stitch on the left-hand needle.

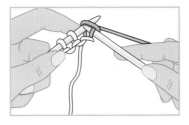

4 Slide the stitch off the left-hand needle. This has formed one knit stitch on the right-hand needle.

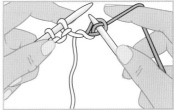

Repeat until all stitches on the left-hand needle have been transferred to the right-hand needle. This is the end of the row. Swap the right-hand needle into your left hand and begin the next row in exactly the same way.

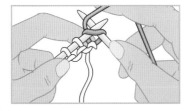

21

Purl Stitch

This is the reverse of the knit stitch. Each stitch is created with a four-step process. Hold the yarn at the front of the work – this is the side facing you.

1 Place the needle with the cast-on stitches in your left hand, insert the right-hand needle into the front of the first stitch on the left-hand needle from right to left.

2 Take the yarn over and around the point of the right-hand needle.

3 Draw the new loop on the right-hand needle through the stitch on the left-hand needle.

4 Slide the stitch off the left-hand needle. This has formed one purl stitch on the right-hand needle.

Repeat these four steps to the end of the row.

GARTER STITCH
Rows of knit stitch build up to form an interlocking fabric, which is called garter stitch (g st). It has ridges on the front and back and is identical from either side, so it is reversible. It forms a flat and fairly thick fabric that does not curl at the edges.

STOCKINETTE STITCH
Making alternate knit and purl rows creates stockinette (stocking) stitch. The knit rows are the right side of the fabric and the purl rows are the wrong side. Instructions for stockinette stitch in knitting patterns can be written as follows:
Row 1 RS Knit
Row 2 Purl
Or alternatively: Work in st st (1 row k, 1 row p), beg with a k row.

Increasing & Decreasing

Many projects are not square or rectangular and therefore need to be shaped by adding or removing stitches. This is called increasing and decreasing.

Increasing Stitches

Make 1 (M1)

This method allows you to create a new stitch in between two existing stitches using the horizontal thread that lies between the stitches. Twisting the stitch prevents a hole appearing and makes your increase practically invisible.

To twist M1 to the left

1 Work to the position of the increase and insert the left-hand needle under the horizontal strand between the next two stitches from front to back.

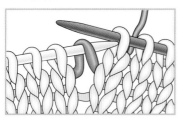

2 Knit this loop through the back to twist it.

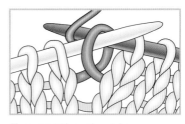

To twist M1 to the right

1 Work to the position of the increase and insert the left-hand needle under the horizontal strand between the next two stitches from back to front.

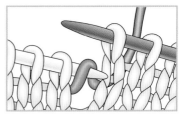

2 Knit this loop through the back to twist it.

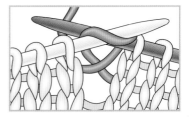

Knit into front and back (Kf&b)

This method is most often used at the edges of the knitted piece. If done neatly, it is virtually invisible within the pattern of stitches. Make sure you keep an even tension as you add the stitches; when you are knitting into the same stitch twice, it is easy to make it very tight and therefore very difficult to knit.

On a knit row Knit the first stitch on the left-hand needle in the usual way, but instead of sliding the stitch off the left-hand needle as you would normally do, still keeping the yarn at the back of the work, knit into the back of the same stitch. Then slide the stitch off the left-hand needle. You now have two stitches on the right-hand needle and have therefore created a stitch.

On a purl row Purl the first stitch on the left-hand needle in the usual way, but instead of sliding the stitch off the left-hand needle as you would normally do, still keeping the yarn at the front of the work, purl into the back of the same stitch. Then slide the stitch off the left-hand needle.

Knit into front, back and front

This increases two stitches instead of one: simply knit into the front, back and then the front again of the same stitch.

Multiple yarn overs (Yos)

These are used to make the holes on the Seed Stitch Set scarf edging (*Textured Knits*).

Yo 4 times Wrap the yarn around the needle four times. On the return row, you must knit into the first loop of the yarn over, purl into the second, knit into the third and purl into the fourth loop.

Yo 5 times Wrap the yarn around the needle five times. On the return row, work into the first four loops of the yarn over as described for yo 4 times, and then knit into the fifth loop.

Decreasing Stitches

Decreasing is used at the ends of rows or within the knitted fabric to reduce the number of stitches being worked on. Here are a number of ways to decrease one stitch.

Knit two stitches together (K2tog)

This is the most straightforward method for decreasing and it does not change the appearance of the knitted fabric apart from making it narrower. Knit to where the decrease is to be made, insert the right-hand needle knitwise through the next two stitches on the left-hand needle. Knit these two stitches together as if they were one stitch.

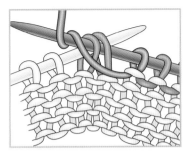

Slip two stitches one at a time (Ssk) or (K2tog tbl)

1 Slip two stitches knitwise one at a time from left-hand needle to right-hand needle (they will be twisted).

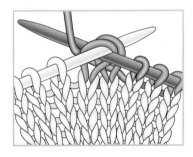

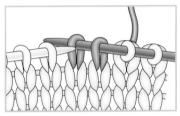

2 Insert the left-hand needle from left to right through the fronts of these two stitches and knit together as one stitch.

Purl two stitches together (P2tog)

Purl to where the decrease is to be made, insert the right-hand needle purlwise through the next two stitches on the left-hand needle. Purl these two stitches together as if they were one stitch.

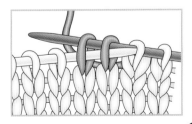

DECREASING TWO STITCHES AT ONCE
There are various ways of decreasing two stitches at once.

K3tog Work as k2tog (page 25), but knit three stitches together instead of two.

P3tog Work as p2tog (page 25), but purl three stitches together instead of two.

K3tog tbl Work as ssk (or k2tog tbl, page 25), but slip three stitches instead of two and knit them together.

Sl2tog-k1-psso
1 Insert the right-hand needle into the next two stitches as if to knit them together, and slip them off together on to the right-hand needle without knitting them. Knit the next stitch.

2 With the tip of the left-hand needle, lift the two slipped stitches together over the knitted stitch and off the needle.

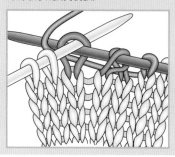
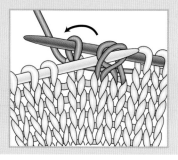

TIP
Always read how to work a decrease very carefully. Some of them have similar abbreviations with only a slight difference between them.

Special Techniques

There are some special techniques that are used for the patterns featured in your box set that need a little more explanation as provided on the next few pages.

Cables

Cables are simply a way of twisting two sets of stitches to form a rope or of carrying stitches across the fabric. A simple cable panel has been worked across the back of the Cable Stitch Wristwarmers (see *Textured Knits*) and the stitches you need to complete this are described in detail below. Use a cable needle to hold the stitches or a double-pointed needle if you find a cable needle too short to hold. If you find working the stitches off the cable needle awkward, replace them on to the left-hand needle to work them.

Cable four front (C4F)

1 Slip the next two stitches from the left-hand needle on to a cable needle and hold at the front of the work.

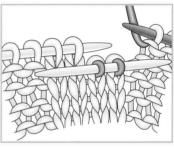

2 Knit the next two stitches on the left-hand needle, then knit the two stitches from the cable needle.

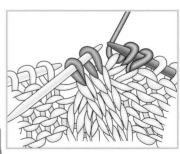

> **TIP**
> Cable needles are short needles pointed at both ends, and some have a kink in the middle to stop the needles falling off.

Cable four back (C4B)

1 Slip the next two stitches from the left-hand needle on to a cable needle and hold at the back of the work.

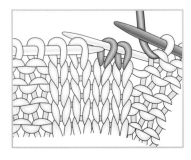

2 Knit the next two stitches on the left-hand needle, then knit the two stitches from the cable needle.

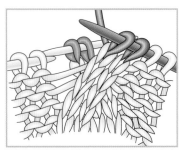

Cross three left (Cr3L)

1 Slip the next two stitches from the left-hand needle on to a cable needle and hold at the front of the work.

2 Purl the next stitch on the left-hand needle, then knit the 2 stitches from the cable needle.

Cross three right (Cr3R)

1 Slip the next stitch from the left-hand needle on to a cable needle and hold at the back of the work.

2 Knit the next two stitches on the left-hand needle, then purl the stitch from the cable needle.

Keeping count

Use a row counter or mark on paper each row worked to keep track of the rows between twists of the cable. To count the rows between twists of a cable, look for the row where you worked the twist; you will be able to identify this by following the path of the yarn from the last stitch of the cable to the first background stitch for a front-cross cable or from the last background stitch to the first stitch of the cable for a back-cross cable. On the row below this there will be no connecting strand of yarn between these same stitches. Count each strand for every row above the twist row.

TIP
A row counter that slides on to the needle helps you to keep track of the row being knitted.

Circular Knitting

Flat knitting is knitted in rows, working back and forth, moving the stitches from one needle to the other. With circular knitting you work in rounds instead of rows; when you reach the end of a row, you simply carry on knitting without turning the work. This produces a tubular piece of fabric. For small tubular items such as gloves, hats and socks double-pointed needles are used. They come in sets of four or five needles. The Ribbed Tube Socks (see *Simple Knits*) requires a set of four needles.

Working on four needles

Cast on the number of stitches required on to one needle. Use the Knitting-on Method (page 18) as the cast-on stitches will need to be fairly loose. Divide the stitches evenly between three needles. When dividing stitches between needles, they should not be too far apart. If the stitches are stretched when the needles are joined, use a shorter needle. Take a spare needle, slip the first group of stitches off knitwise on

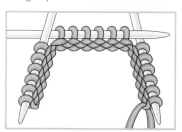

to this needle, and then repeat with a second needle. The final group of stitches remains on the needle on which they were originally cast on. Make sure that the cast on edge is facing inwards and is not twisted.

Bring the three needles together to form a triangle. Place a marker to indicate the end of the round (slip this on every round). Taking your fourth needle, knit the first cast-on stitch, pulling up the yarn to avoid a gap between the first and third needle. Knit the remaining stitches from the first needle. The first needle is now empty and becomes the working needle.

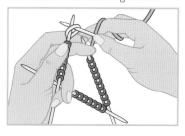

Knit the stitches from the second needle onto the working needle. The second needle is now empty and becomes the working needle. Knit the stitches from the third needle onto the working needle. You have now completed one round. Working the first round can be awkward; the needles not being used tend to dangle and get in the way. After a few rounds the emerging fabric helps to hold the needles in place. Continue working in this way to produce a piece of tubular

Intarsia

Intarsia is the technique of colour knitting used to create the flower heads on the Intarsia Flower Bag (see *Embelllished Knits*). Each area of colour worked within the knitted piece is worked with a separate ball of yarn called a bobbin, so each flower has a separate bobbin and so does each area of background colour between them. As you work, the yarns are twisted where they meet so the blocks of colour are held together.

Bobbins

When you knit with more than one colour of yarn, particularly for the intarsia method of colourwork, it helps to keep the yarns separate on bobbins to prevent them tangling and to make working easier. You can buy plastic bobbins and wrap a small amount of yarn on to each. Alternatively you can hand-wind your own small bobbins. Hand-winding a small bobbin is quick and easy.

Hand-winding a bobbin

Leaving a long end, wind the yarn in a figure-of-eight around your thumb and little finger. Cut the yarn and use this cut end to tie a knot around the middle of the bobbin. Use the long end to pull the yarn from the middle of the bobbin. Use the long end to pull the yarn from the middle of the bobbin.

Joining in a new colour

1 Insert the tip of the right-hand needle into the next stitch, place the cut end (4in/10cm from the end) of the new colour over the old colour and over the tip of the right-hand needle.

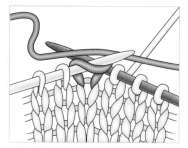

2 Take the working end of the new colour and knit the next stitch, pulling the cut end off the needle over the working end as the stitch is formed so it is not knitted in. Hold the cut end down against the back of the work.

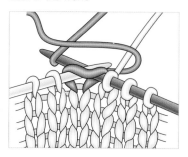

Once you've joined in all the colours that you need across the row, on the return row twist the yarns to join the blocks of colour together. When you change colour, always pick up the new colour from under the old yarn.

Twisting yarns on a knit row

Insert the tip of the right-hand needle into the next stitch, pull the old colour to the left, pick up the new colour and bring it up behind the old colour. Knit the next stitch. The two yarns are twisted together.

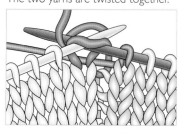

Twisting yarns on a purl row

Insert the tip of the right-hand needle into the next stitch, pull the old colour to the left, pick up the new colour and bring it up behind the old colour. Purl the next stitch. The two yarns are twisted together.

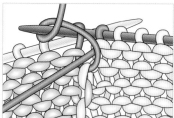

Working from charts

Intarsia patterns are worked from charts. One square represents one stitch and a line of stitches represents one row. The rows are numbered: knit rows (RS rows) are odd numbers and are read from right to left; purl rows (WS rows) are even numbers and are read from left to right. Start knitting from the bottom right-hand corner of the chart at row 1.

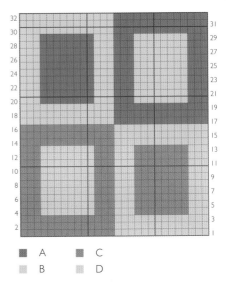

A   C
B   D

Sewing in loose ends

Finish a piece of intarsia knitting by sewing in and cutting off any stray ends. Where the two colours are twisted together, you will see a line of loops. Using a large-eyed tapestry needle, darn in the end along this line in one direction and then back again for a few stitches. Block the piece (see page 35) and push any distorted stitches back into place with the end of a tapestry needle.

Decorative Techniques

There are several different ways of embellishing the projects featured in your *How to Knit* box set and these are covered here.

Beads and Sequins

This simple technique is ideal for adding a large number of beads or sequins, such as on the Sequinned Knitted Throw (*Textured Knits*). Unlike other methods of beaded knitting, you don't have to thread all the beads onto the yarn before you begin.

Place bead or sequin (PB)

1 Insert crochet hook through hole in the sequin and hook the next stitch off the left-hand needle and through the sequin.

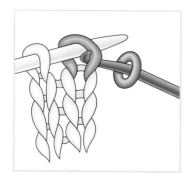

2 Place the stitch onto the right-hand needle without working it.

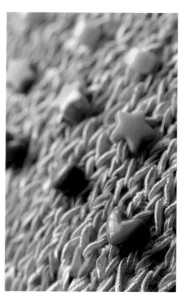

Other Touches

From simple embroidery to pompom trims there are a few other decorative touches you will need to know to finish the featured projects.

Backstitch

Use embroidery thread, tapestry wool or knitting yarn, and a large-eyed blunt tapestry needle. Weave the thread through a few knitted stitches at the beginning and end of the embroidery to secure it. To begin, bring the needle up at A. In one movement, take the needle down at B and up at C. Take it down at A and up at D, down at C and up at E, down at D and up at F. Work your embroidery loosely; if it is too tight, it will make the fabric pucker.

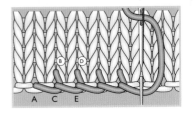

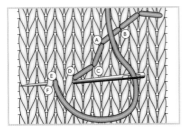

Buttonhole stitch

This is used for the Stockinette Strip Bag (*Simple Knits*) to reinforce the button loop. Bring the needle out at A. In one movement, take it down at B and back up at C, looping the thread under the needle tip. The next stitch is worked to the right, down at D and up at E. The horizontal threads should lie on the fabric edge.

Pompoms

1 Cut two circles of thick cardboard that are slightly larger than the diameter of the finished pompom. Cut a circle from the centre of each circle half this size. Wind yarn around until the centre hole is filled.

2 Carefully cut through the yarn and gently ease the discs apart.

3 Take a small piece of yarn and tie it firmly around the middle. Ease the circles off and fluff up. Trim to give an even shape, leaving the two yarn ends for securing to your knitting.

Finishing Techniques

Here are all the finishing techniques you might need to complete the projects. Not all will be required, so just refer to the ones you need.

Blocking

The process of pinning and pressing knitted pieces is called blocking and it is important to make your finished projects look as good as possible. First sew in all yarn ends, then steam or wet press as appropriate to your yarn.

Steam pressing

This method is used for natural yarns or those with a high wool content. Yarns with a high synthetic content will not stand the high temperatures of steam pressing, and care should be taken with long-haired fibres such as mohair and angora and items with textured stitches to ensure the fibres are not matted or the pattern flattened by the steaming process. Always check the information on the ball band before pressing and test out how your fabric will react on your gauge square first if you have any doubts.

Use rustproof large-headed pins to pin out each piece to its exact measurements, wrong side up, on your ironing board or blocking board. You can make your own board from a large piece of chip board or similar material covered with a layer of foam and then a layer of checked or gingham fabric. This will give you lines to guide you when pinning out your knitting. Staple the fabric to the reverse of the board. Lay a clean cotton cloth over your knitting to protect it.

Set the iron to an appropriate heat setting for your yarn. Hold the iron close to the surface of the knitting and allow the steam to permeate. Do not press the iron onto the knitted fabric. Remove the cloth and allow your knitting to dry thoroughly before unpinning.

Wet pressing

This alternative method is suitable for synthetics and fancy yarns. Pin out your knitting to the exact measurements on your ironing or pressing board as before. Wet a clean cloth and squeeze out the excess water until it is just damp. Place the cloth over your knitting and leave to dry. Remove the cloth when it is completely dry and ensure the knitted pieces are also dry before unpinning them.

Sewing Up

There are different methods for sewing your knitted pieces together depending on the finish you are trying to achieve. If possible, sew up your items with the same yarn you used to knit them. If the yarn is very thick, highly textured or breaks easily, use a plain yarn in a matching colour. Use a tapestry needle and keep the length of the yarn you use to sew up at reasonable lengths, so it does not fray as it continually passes through the fabric: 18in (45cm) lengths are most suitable.

Mattress stitch

Use mattress stitch to produce an almost invisible seam. This stitch is worked from the right side of the fabric, allowing you to match patterns and shaping details. To join two pieces of stockinette stitch lay the pieces to be joined out flat, right sides up and together. Secure the pieces together by bringing the needle through from back to front at the bottom of the right-hand piece, taking the needle through the left-hand piece from back to front and back under the right-hand piece and out at the front. This makes a figure-of-eight with the yarn and gives a nice start to the seam.

Take the needle across and under the left-hand piece and bring it through to the front from the same hole as the securing stitch. Now take the needle back to the right-hand piece

and bring it up under the horizontal strands of the two stitches above the first entry point. Take the needle back to the left-hand piece, insert the needle back into the stitch that the yarn is emerging from and take the needle up under the next two horizontal strands. Pull up the stitches to tighten them and draw the two edges together. Continue working from side to side in this way, tightening the yarn every few stitches but not so tight as to pucker the fabric.

Backstitch

This seaming stitch is worked from the wrong side of the fabric and is used when you require a strong seam, but don't have to match the stitches row for row. The way the pieces are joined creates a seam allowance, which can be bulky, so you should sew your seam as close to the edge of the pieces as possible. Backstitch is often used to seam cushions and join different pieces of knitted fabric.

Place the pieces to be joined, right sides together and pin in place. Bring the needle through from the back to the front, one knitted stitch down from the starting edge. Insert the needle one knitted stitch back and bring it out one knitted stitch ahead. Pull the yarn through to tighten and form a stitch. Repeat this step as you continue along the seam, making one backstitch cover one knitted stitch.

Overcasting

Overcasting creates a narrow seam that is also flat, so it is a useful method of joining knitted pieces. It is usually worked from the wrong side. Pin the pieces to be joined with their right sides together, matching the stitches exactly. Join the yarn securely at the edge of the two seams. Work along the seam taking the needle under the strands at the edge of the seam, between the matched 'bumps', from back to front. After each stitch, tighten the yarn gently over the knitted edge. Keep the tension of each stitch the same. The join between the two pieces should be neat and flat with no bulky ridge.

Flat seam

Use this for joining on an edging, such as the one on the scarf in the Seed Stitch Set (*Textured Knits*). Lay the edging on top of the main fabric, just covering the edge. Sew through both thicknesses, using a small running stitch. Do not pull the stitches too tightly or the fabrics will pucker.

Crochet Edging

A crochet edging is worked around the edge of the knitted cuff in Ballet Slipper Bling (*Embellished Knits*). Decide where you are going to start the crochet round; insert the crochet hook underneath both the horizontal strands of yarn at the top of one knitted stitch. Make a slip knot in the working end of the yarn and place the loop of the slip knot onto the hook. Pull this loop through the knitted fabric and begin the single crochet.

single crochet (sc)

1 To make the stitch, insert your hook under the top two strands of the stitch. Wrap the yarn over the hook and pull the yarn through.

2 Then wrap the yarn over the hook again and pull it through both the loops on the hook. This forms one single crochet stitch.

Troubleshooting

Don't worry – all knitters make a mistake sometimes.
Here are some of the more common mistakes made and
instructions on how to correct them.

Dropped Stitches

Dropped stitches have fallen off the
needle and unravelled down, creating
a ladder effect in the fabric. This is
easily rectified if you notice it quickly,
so take time to check your knitting
every few rows.

Knit stitch dropped one row below

Make sure that the horizontal strand
of yarn is behind the dropped stitch.
Insert the right-hand needle into the
dropped stitch from front to back
and under the horizontal strand of
yarn behind it. Insert the left-hand
needle into the dropped stitch and
lift the stitch over the horizontal
strand and off the right-hand needle.

Purl stitch dropped one row below

Make sure that the horizontal strand
of yarn is in front of the dropped
stitch. Insert the right-hand needle
into the dropped stitch from the
back and under the horizontal strand
of yarn in front of it. Insert the left-
hand needle into the dropped stitch
and lift the stitch over the horizontal
strand and off the right-hand needle.

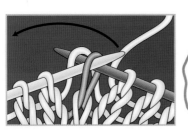

TIP

*When returning to your knitting after
a long break, undo a few rows to
eliminate unsightly ridges that can be
caused by stretched stitches – a danger
when leaving your work on the needles
for any length of time.*

Stitch dropped several rows below

To pick up a knit stitch, insert a crochet hook through the front of the stitch, catch the yarn strand immediately above and pull it through the stitch. Repeat for all strands in the ladder up to the top of the knitting and slip the stitch back onto the left-hand needle.

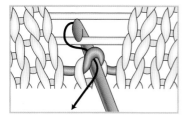

To pick up a purl stitch, follow the instructions for a knit stitch but work from the wrong side of the fabric.

Unravelling one row

If you have made an error in the stitches that you have just worked on the right needle, for example knitting when you should have purled, there is no need to take the work off the needle to unravel back to that point. Unravel the knitting stitch by stitch

back to the error. With the front of the fabric facing you, put the left-hand needle into the stitch below the stitch on the right-hand needle, drop the stitch off the right-hand needle and pull the yarn. Repeat this for each stitch until you reach the error. Purl stitches are unravelled in the same way.

Unravelling several rows

Find the row that you want to take your knitting back to, which should be just below the error. With the right side of the fabric facing you, take a knitting needle that is smaller than the needles you are working with and weave it in and out of each stitch on the row. Work from right to left across the whole row, passing the needle under the right-hand and over the left-hand sides of the stitch. Remove the original needle from the top of the fabric. Gently pull the yarn away from the stitches and they will unravel, one by one. Continue in this way until you reach the smaller needle. Transfer the stitches on this needle to a needle of the correct size, making sure that you do not twist the stitches in this process, and continue knitting.

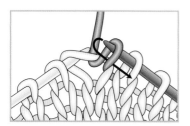

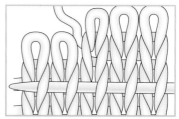

Yarn Misadventures

Below is guidance for dealing with some other common problems experienced by new knitters.

Running out of yarn

Join in new balls of yarn at the beginning of a row or at a seam edge, so that you will be able to weave in the yarn ends neatly. Drop the old yarn and knit the next few stitches with the new yarn. Tie the ends at the beginning of the row together securely so the ends do not slip out and unravel your work. When you have finished knitting, undo the knot and weave one end up the edge of the fabric for a few inches, doubling back for a few stitches to secure it. Do not pull too tightly and distort the fabric. Weave the other end in the opposite direction in the same way.

TIP

To work a row of stockinette stitch you will need yarn measuring four times the width of the knitting, more for textured and cable patterns. If in doubt start a new ball.

Split yarn

When you are working fast, it can be easy to split a strand of yarn or to miss a strand when using several strands together. Always unravel and rework the stitch, otherwise it will be visible on the finished fabric.

Incomplete stitches

This can happen if you wrap the yarn around the needle but do not pull it through the old stitch to form a new one. You can work the stitch properly following the instructions for how to deal with dropped stitches.

Snagged stitches

Use a tapestry needle to ease the extra yarn back through any distorted stitches, one by one, beginning with the stitch closest to the snagged area.

Aftercare

It is always best to be ultra-cautious when washing hand-knitted items because there is nothing worse than ruining something that has taken so many hours of hard work. You may like to keep a ball band and a small sample of the yarn used in each project in a notebook. The ball band will give specific care instructions, as different types of yarn require different treatments.

Index

abbreviations 12–13
aftercare 40
alpaca 4

backstitch 34, 36–7
beads 33
binding off 19–20
blocking 35
bobbins 30
buttonhole stitch 34

cables 27–8
cashmere 4
casting on 16–17, 16–18
charts 15, 32
circular knitting 29
cotton 4
crochet edging 37

crochet hooks 9
decreasing stitches 25–6
dropped stitches 38–9

gauge (tension) 10–11

incomplete stitches 40
increasing stitches 23–4
intarsia 30–2

keeping count 28
knit stitch 21, 38–9

linen 4

mattress stitch 36

measurements 11, 14
mohair 4–5

needles, types/ sizes 9

overcasting 37

patterns 10–15
picking up stitches 20
pompoms 34
pressing 35
purl stitch 22, 38–9

seams 36–7
sequins 33
sewing up 36–7
silk 5
slip knots 17

snagged stitches 40
stitch charts 15
stockinette stitch 22
synthetic fibres 5

troubleshooting 38–40

unravelling rows 39

wool 5

yarns 4–8
  colour 8
  measuring 11
  misadventures 40
  ply 7
  texture 8, 11
  thickness 7
  types 4–5
  weight 6–7

HOW TO KNIT BOX SET
A DAVID & CHARLES BOOK
Copyright © David & Charles Limited 2010

Project designs copyright © Louise Butt & Kirstie McLeod, Claire Crompton, Jenny Hill
All rights reserved. No part of this publication may be reproduced, stored in a retrieval system, or transmitted, in any form or by any means, electronic or mechanical, by photocopying, recording or otherwise, without prior permission in writing from the publisher.

The designs in this book are copyright and must not be made for resale.

The project designers and publisher have made every effort to ensure that all the instructions in the book are accurate and safe, and therefore cannot accept liability for any resulting injury, damage or loss to persons or property, however it may arise.

Names of manufacturers, yarn ranges and other products are provided for the information of readers, with no intention to infringe copyright or trademarks.

A catalogue record for this book is available from the British Library.

ISBN-13: 978-0-7153-3782-0
ISBN-10: 0-7153-3782-3

Printed in China by RR Donnelley
for David & Charles, Brunel House, Newton Abbot, Devon

Knit stitch

Continental method *(yarn in the left hand)*

In this method the right-hand needle moves to catch the yarn; the yarn is held at the back of the work (the side facing away from you) and is released by the index finger of the left hand. This knit stitch is made up of four steps.

1 Hold the needle with the cast on stitches in your left hand and the yarn over your left index finger. Insert the right-hand needle into the front of the stitch from left to right.

3 Pull the new loop on the right-hand needle through the stitch on the left-hand needle, using the right index finger to hold the new loop if needed.

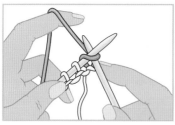

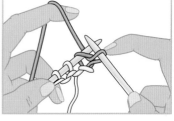

2 Move the right-hand needle down and across the back of the yarn.

4 Slip the stitch off the left-hand needle. One knit stitch is completed.

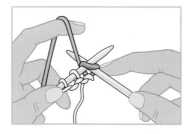

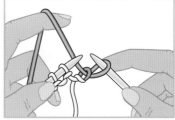

How To Knit:
Textured Knits

Contents

Introduction	2
NOVELTY KNIT BAG	4
TEXTURED STITCH THROW	8
SEED STITCH SET	18
CABLE STITCH WRISTWARMERS	28
Abbreviations	36
Yarn Details	38
Suppliers	40
Other Books	41

Introduction

There are many different ways to bring texture into your knitting, from the yarns you choose to work with to the knitted stitches you choose to use. This book features projects to help you begin to explore textural knitting.

A simple yet glamorous bag illustrates perfectly how clever yarn choice can bring great texture to your knitting. A cosy throw introduces you to a few knitted stitches, and working panels in four different stitch patterns will give you plenty of practice. Seed (moss) stitch is such an easy textured stitch to achieve, and the beret, scarf and corsage set is perfect for getting to grips with this lovely pattern. And, finally, a snug pair of wristwarmers will induce you to try your hand at the twists and turns of a cable pattern.

Also squeezed in are extra ideas for varying the patterns included, so look out for the Knit Twos, Threes or even more. For the specific yarn details for all of the projects featured, see pages 38–39.

Novelty knit bag

Sometimes all the texture you need comes from the yarn you choose. Take, for example, this fabulously vibrant furry yarn. Shot through with filaments of silky and metallic thread, it is very soft and multi-tonal, which gives this particular shade of red real depth. Such yarns have most impact when used in small amounts, and this small bag shows it off to its best. The purse is made in two triangle shapes. The back piece is knitted with an additional flap which hangs down over the front to keep it closed. And, as if it weren't extravagant-looking enough, the bag is also trimmed with beads and pompoms.

yarn
2 × 1¾oz (50g) balls of light-weight (DK) novelty yarn with wisps and fibres

needles and notions
- 1 pair of size 5 (3.75mm) needles
- Darning needle
- 20in (50cm) toning fabric for lining
- Long necklace in toning colour to make handle, or gold chain, or a selection of beads
- 4 small pompoms (optional)
- Sewing thread

size
8in (20cm) wide and 10½in (27cm) long (at widest and longest points)

gauge
24 sts and 30 rows to 4in (10cm) square over garter stitch using size 5 (3.75mm) needles

TIP
The filaments of silky and metallic thread make this yarn extremely tactile.

For furry yarns there is no point using fancy stitches, as they are completely lost behind the tufts and fluffs.

Knit your bag

Front

Using size 5 (3.75mm) needles, cast on 41 sts.

Knit 40 rows garter stitch (every row knit).

Row 41 K2tog, knit to last 2 sts, k2tog. 39 sts.

Knit a further 4 rows.

Row 46 K2tog, knit to last 2 sts, k2tog. 37 sts.

Knit a further 4 rows.

Row 51 K2tog, knit to last 2 sts, k2tog. 35 sts.

Knit a further 4 rows.

Row 56 K2tog, knit to last 2 sts, k2tog. 33 sts.

Knit a further 2 rows.

Repeat these last 3 rows 14 times. 5 sts.

Row 101 K2tog, K1, K2tog. 3 sts.

Cast off rem 3 sts.

Back (starting with flap)

Using size 5 (3.75mm) needles, cast on 3 sts.

Knit 1 row.

Row 2 Inc 1, knit to end, inc 1. 5 sts.

Knit a further 2 rows.

Rep these last 3 rows 19 times. 41 sts. This completes the flap.

Cont the back as for front piece.

Making up

Darn in any loose ends. Place the knitted pieces under a damp cloth and steam the knitting gently with an iron. Using each knitted piece as a template, cut two pieces of lining. Sew the sides of the lining together and then slipstitch the hems to the knitted piece on the front edge and around the flap's point. Sew the knitted pieces together.

Measure the length of your desired handle. If using a chain handle or ready-made beaded necklace, use the hooks to sew onto the bag, or thread contrasting beads onto double lengths of strong embroidery thread and create your own necklace to use as a handle. Sew on securely, darning in any loose ends.

Create three beaded lengths, with optional pompom ends, and attach to the point of the flap securely. Hide the 'sewing on' with a further pompom or glass bead. These beaded lengths are decorative, but also weight the flap down to keep the bag closed and safe.

TIP
This pattern would look very glamorous knitted in black yarn with gold metallic highlights, complete with a chain handle.

Textured stitch throw

This cosy throw gives you an opportunity to try out some wonderfully knitted stitches. It is made up of eight panels of varying widths that are knitted separately and sewn together at the end, and it features four textured stitches: dimple stitch, giant dimple stitch, blind buttonhole stitch and hexagon stitch. These patterns are made by slipping stitches to make tucks and depressions in the fabric. Denim yarn is particularly good for holding textured stitches, and different makes in a range of blues from light denim to very dark navy denim have been used. Specific instructions for changing yarns in a panel have not been given; just use them randomly to create a shaded, textural fabric.

yarn
37 x 1¾oz (50g) ball of light-weight (DK) denim cotton yarn (average 102yd/93m per ball) in four shades of denim ranging from light to dark

needles and notions
1 pair of size 7 (4.5mm) needles

size
After washing: 56in (142cm) wide and 52in (132cm) long

gauge
19 sts and 26 rows to 4in (10cm) measured over st st (1 row k, 1 row p) using size 7 (4.5mm) needles

SPECIAL ABBREVIATIONS
Sl 2 [3:4:5] wyif Slip 2 [3:4:5] sts purlwise with yarn in front of work
Sl 2 [3:4:5] wyib Slip 2 [3:4:5] sts purlwise with yarn at back of work

TIP
Use the denim yarn that is designed to shrink and fade after washing.

dark navy denim

navy denim

indigo denim

mid-blue denim

light blue denim

The denim yarn shows off the deeply textured relief stitches.

Eight different panels are worked in four different textured stitches: dimple stitch (panels A and B), giant dimple stitch (panels C and D), blind buttonhole stitch (panels E and F, and hexagon stitch (panels G and H).

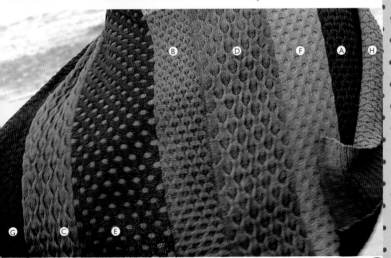

Knit your throw

Use the different shades and makes of denim randomly for each panel. Knit some panels in one yarn, and use two or three yarns to knit other panels.

Dimple stitch panels

Gathering st: take yarn to back as though to knit, insert needle from below under 3 strands, k the next st, bring the st out under the strands

Panel A

Using size 7 (4.5mm) needles, cast on 41 sts.
Knit 1 row.
Purl 1 row.
Row 1 (RS) K.
Row 2 P1, sl 3 wyif, * p3, sl 3 wyif; rep from * to last st, p1.
Row 3 K1, sl 3 wyib, *k3, sl 3 wyib; rep from * to last st, k1.
Row 4 As row 2.
Row 5 K.
Row 6 P.
Row 7 K.
Row 8 P2, gathering st, *p5, gathering st; rep from * to last 2 sts, p2.
Row 9 K.
Row 10 P4, *sl 3 wyif, p3; rep from * to last st, p1.
Row 11 K4, *sl 3 wyif, k3; rep from * to last st, k1.
Row 12 As row 10.
Row 13 K.
Row 14 P.
Row 15 K.

Row 16 P5, *gathering st, p5; rep from * to end.
Repeat these 16 rows until panel measures approx 63in (160cm) from beg, ending with row 8 or row 16 of pattern.
Knit 1 row.
Purl 1 row.
Bind off.

Panel B

Using size 7 (4.5mm) needles, cast on 29 sts and work as given for Panel A.

12

Giant dimple stitch panels

Gathering st: take yarn to back as though to knit, insert needle from below under 5 strands, k the next st, bring the st out under the strands

Panel C

Using size 7 (4.5mm) needles, cast on 37 sts.
Knit 1 row.
Purl 1 row.
Row 1 (RS) K.
Row 2 P1, sl 5 wyif, *p5, sl 5 wyif; rep from * to last st, p1.

Row 3 K1, sl 5 wyib, *k5, sl 5 wyib; rep from * to last st, k1.
Row 4 As row 2.
Row 5 As row 3.
Row 6 As row 2.
Row 7 K.
Row 8 P.
Row 9 K.
Row 10 P.
Row 11 K
Row 12 P3, gathering st, *p9, gathering st; rep from * to last 3 sts, p3.
Row 13 K.
Row 14 P6, *sl 5 wyif, p5; rep from * to last st, p1.
Row 15 K6, *sl 5 wyif, k5; rep from * to last st, k1.
Row 16 As row 14.
Row 17 As row 15.
Row 18 As row 14.
Row 19 K.
Row 20 P.
Row 21 K.
Row 22 P.
Row 23 K.
Row 24 P8, gathering st, *p9, gathering st; rep from * to last 8 sts, p8.
Repeat these 24 rows until panel measures approx 63in (160cm) from beg, ending with row 12 or row 24 of pattern.
Knit 1 row.
Purl 1 row.
Bind off.

Panel D

Using size 7 (4.5mm) needles, cast on 47 sts and work as given for Panel C.

Blind buttonhole stitch panels
Panel E
(Uses two shades of denim; dark A and light B).

Using size 7 (4.5mm) needles and A, cast on 54 sts.
Row 1 (WS) Using A, knit.
Row 2 Using A, purl.
Row 3 Using A, knit.
Row 4 Using A, purl.
Row 5 Using A, knit.
Row 6 Using B, k1, sl 4 wyib, *k4, sl 4 wyib; rep from * to last st, k1.
Row 7 Using B, P1, sl 4 wyif, *p4, sl 4 wyif; rep from * to last st, p1.
Row 8 Using B, as row 6.
Row 9 Using B, as row 7.
Row 10 Using A, as row 6.
Row 11 Using A, knit.
Row 12 Using A, purl.
Row 13 Using A, knit.
Row 14 Using A, purl.
Row 15 Using A, knit.
Row 16 Using B, k5, sl 4 wyib, *k4, sl 4 wyib; rep from * to last 5 sts, k5.
Row 17 Using B, p5, sl 4 wyif, *p4, sl 4 wyif; rep from * to last 5 sts, p5.
Row 18 Using B, as row 16.
Row 19 Using B, as row 17.
Row 20 Using A, as row 16.
Repeat these 20 rows until panel measures approx 63in (160cm) from beg, ending with row 5 or row 15 of pattern. Bind off.

Panel F
Using size 7 (4.5mm) needles, cast on 38 sts and work as given for Panel E, using one colour throughout.

Hexagon stitch panels

Panel G

Using size 7 (4.5mm) needles, cast on 32 sts.

Row 1 (RS) P.
Row 2 K.
Row 3 K3, sl 2 wyib, *k6, sl 2 wyib; rep from * to last 3 sts, k3.
Row 4 P3, sl 2 wyif, *p6, sl 2 wyif; rep from * to last 3 sts, k3.
Row 5 As row 3.
Row 6 As row 4.
Row 7 P.
Row 8 K.
Row 9 K7, sl 2 wyib, *k6, sl 2 wyib; rep from * to last 7 sts, k7.
Row 10 P7, sl 2 wyif, *p6, sl 2 wyif; rep from * to last 7 sts, p7.
Row 11 As row 9.
Row 12 As row 10.

Repeat these 12 rows until panel measures approx 63in (160cm) from beg, ending with row 6 or row 12 of pattern.
Purl 1 row.
Knit 1 row.
Bind off.

Panel H

Using size 7 (4.5mm) needles, cast on 48 sts and work as given for Panel G.

Making up

Sew in all ends neatly.
Wind off a couple of small
skeins of yarn to be used
for sewing up. Wash the
panels and skeins (put
the skeins in a small fabric
bag to prevent tangling in
the machine) according
to instructions on the ball
bands.

After washing, some panels
may have shrunk more
than others. Find the
shortest panel and pull
back the other panels to
match its length. Using
yarn from the skein, join
the panels together in a
random order.

TIP
*You could easily alter the
size of the throw by knitting
more or fewer panels.*

Knit Two

Rework this throw in soft, pastel shades for a bedroom and trim it with a delicate floral braid. Yarns used include light-weight (DK) cashmere/wool in soft pink and aqua, pale yellow cotton and spring green silk/cotton.

Knit Three

Create a warmer wool fabric taking inspiration from richly coloured, vibrant hedgerow berries. Yarns used include light-weight (DK) wool in dark plum, soft raspberry and blackberry, and silk/wool in rich berry red and dark raspberry.

Seed stitch set

This three-piece set of scarf, beret and corsage is worked in a luxurious wool and cashmere mix yarn in a deep, rich shade of red that shows off the texture of the seed (moss) stitch beautifully. Knit the whole set or pick out individual pieces to make up your own look. The scarf and beret are knitted using two strands of the yarn, to produce a lush, richly textured fabric. As the corsage needs more precise shaping it is worked in one strand of yarn, with the petals worked in garter stitch. The lacy edging on the scarf provides an attractive flounce of detail.

scarf

The fancy ends of this scarf can be threaded through the keyhole to keep the scarf snug around your neck even on the windiest of days. It is worked in seed (moss) stitch using two strands of yarn together, so is very quick to knit. The large holes in the edgings are made with multiple yarnovers (yos) and then several stitches are worked into them (see Increasing Stitches, Basics, page 24).

you will need

yarn
3 x 1¾oz (50g) balls of light-weight (DK) wool/cashmere mix yarn (142yd/130m per ball) in claret red

needles
1 pair of size 10 (6mm) needles

size
5½in (14cm) wide by 40in (101.5cm) long

gauge
16 sts and 26 rows to 4in (10cm) measured over seed (moss) stitch using size 10 (6mm) needles and two strands of yarn together

knit note
Two yarns are used together to make a thicker yarn. Work through both yarns for each stitch

TIP
This set would look equally good worked in a light-weight (DK) pure wool or wool tweed.

Knit your scarf

Using size 10 (6mm) needles and two strands of yarn together, cast on 20 sts loosely.

Row 1 RS *K1, p1; rep from * to end.
Row 2 *P1, k1; rep from * to end.
These 2 rows form seed (moss) stitch and are repeated.
Cont in patt until scarf measures 4in (10cm), ending with a WS row.
Divide for keyhole:
Next Row Patt 10 sts, join in a new yarn (of two strands) and use this to patt to end.
Working both sides at the same time, work in patt until keyhole measures 3in (7.5cm), ending with a WS row.
Next Row Patt across all 20 sts (joining two sides into one again).
Cut off second yarn.
Cont in patt until scarf measures 32in (81.5cm), ending with a WS row.
Bind off loosely in patt.

Edging (make 2)

Using size 10 (6mm) needles and two strands of yarn together, cast on 13 sts loosely.
Foundation Row 1 K3, p10.
Foundation Row 2 K2, (yo) 4 times, k2tog, k6, turn.
Row 1 P7, (k1, p1) twice into 4-yo loop, p2.
Row 2 K16.
Row 3 K3, p13.
Row 4 K2, (yo) 5 times, k2tog, k9 and turn.
Row 5 P10, (k1, p1, k1, p1, k1) into 5-yo loop, p2.

Row 6 K20.
Row 7 K3, p17.
Row 8 Bind off 7 sts, k2 (including last st used in bind-off), (yo) 4 times, k2tog, k6 and turn.
These 8 rows form the edging and are repeated. Cont in patt until edging fits across end of scarf, ending with row 7 of patt.
Bind off loosely.

Making up

Sew in all ends. Press according to instructions on ball band. Sew an edging onto each end of the scarf.

Beret

Using two strands of yarn together, the stylish beret is worked in seed (moss) stitch. The k1, p1 rib fits snugly around your head. After the rib, you increase stitches using M1 (see Increasing Stitches, *Basics*, page 23), then shape the crown using p3tog and k3tog (see Decreasing Stitches, *Basics*, page 26) so that the seed (moss) stitch pattern isn't interrupted.

you will need

yarn
2 × 1¾oz (50g) balls of light-weight (DK) wool/cashmere mix yarn (142yd/130m per ball) in claret red

needles
• 1 pair of size 8 (5mm) needles
• 1 pair of size 10 (6mm) needles

size
To fit head circumference 20 [22]in (51 [56]cm)

gauge
16 sts and 26 rows to 4in (10cm) measured over seed (moss) stitch using size 10 (6mm) needles and two strands of yarn together

knit note
Two yarns are used together to make a thicker yarn. Make sure that you work through both yarns for each stitch

TIP

Choose a yarn that is smooth rather than textured; otherwise, the seed (moss) stitch will not be clearly defined.

Knit your beret

Using size 8 (5mm) needles and two strands of yarn together, cast on 68 [76] sts.
Row 1 *K1, p1; rep from * to end. This row forms the rib.
Work a further 4 rows in rib.
Inc Row Rib 4 [6], (rib 1 [2], M1, rib 2, M1) 20 [16] times, rib 4 [6]. 108 sts.
Change to size 10 (6mm) needles.
Row 1 RS *K1, p1; rep from * to end.
Row 2 *P1, k1; rep from * to end.
These 2 rows form seed (moss) stitch and are repeated. Work a further 20 rows in patt.

Shape top
Row 23 K1, p1, k1, *p3tog, (k1, p1) 3 times, k3tog, (p1, k1) 3 times; rep from * to last 15 sts, p3tog, (k1, p1) 3 times, k3tog, p1, k1, p1. 84 sts.
Patt 7 rows.
Row 31 K1, p1, *k3tog, (p1, k1) twice, p3tog, (k1, p1) twice; rep from * to last 12 sts, k3tog, (p1, k1) twice, p3tog, k1, p1. 60 sts.
Patt 7 rows.
Row 39 K1, *p3tog, k1, p1, k3tog, p1, k1; rep from * to last 9 sts, p3tog, k1, p1, k3tog, p1. 36 sts.
Patt 3 rows.
Row 43 *K1, p1, k1, p3tog; rep from * to end. 24 sts.
Patt 1 row.

Row 45 *K3tog, p1; rep from * to end. 12 sts.
Purl 1 row.
Cut yarn and thread through rem sts. Pull up tight and fasten off.

Making up

Sew in all ends. Press according to instructions on ball band. Join back seam.

Corsage

Each of the six petals is knitted separately; they are then joined at the base to produce a large bloom. The petal is shaped by working three times into one st – knit into front, back and front (see Increasing Stitches, *Basics*, page 24) and decreased using ssk, k2tog and sl2tog-k1-psso (see Decreasing Stitches, *Basics*, page 26). The centre is filled with sequins and beads.

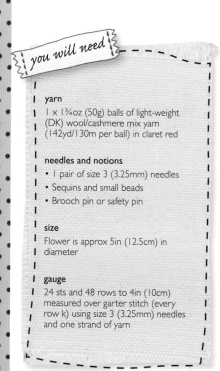

you will need

yarn
- 1 x 1¾oz (50g) balls of light-weight (DK) wool/cashmere mix yarn (142yd/130m per ball) in claret red

needles and notions
- 1 pair of size 3 (3.25mm) needles
- Sequins and small beads
- Brooch pin or safety pin

size
Flower is approx 5in (12.5cm) in diameter

gauge
24 sts and 48 rows to 4in (10cm) measured over garter stitch (every row k) using size 3 (3.25mm) needles and one strand of yarn

TIP
Knit the corsage in a bright cotton yarn and pin it to the beret, worked in a contrasting cotton/silk mix yarn for warmer days.

Knit your corsage

Petal (make 6)

Using size 3 (3.25mm) needles and single strand of yarn, cast on 3 sts and knit 1 row.

Row 1 RS K1, (k into front, back and front) into next st, k1. 5 sts.
Row 2 Knit.
Row 3 K2, (k into front, back and front) into next st, k2. 7 sts.
Row 4 Knit.
Row 5 K3, (k into front, back and front) into next st, k3. 9 sts.
Row 6 Knit.
Row 7 K4, (k into front, back and front) into next st, k4. 11 sts.

Knit 5 rows.
Row 13 K1, ssk, k5, k2tog, k1. 9 sts.
Knit 5 rows.
Row 19 K1, ssk, k3, k2tog, k1. 7 sts.
Knit 3 rows.
Row 23 K1, ssk, k1, k2tog, k1. 5 sts.
Knit 3 rows.
Row 27 K1, sl2tog-k1-psso, k1. 3 sts.
Knit 1 row.
Row 29 Sl2tog-k1-psso. 1 st.
Cut yarn and thread through rem st.

Making up

Sew in all ends. Fold each petal in half (with RS together) at the base and sew the side edges together for ½in (1.5cm). Place the petals side by side and run a gathering thread through each to join. Pull the thread tight and repeat through all petals again to form a circle. Pull the thread tight so the flower becomes dish-shaped. Secure the thread. Fill the centre with sequins and beads, sewing the beads onto the top of the sequins. Sew a brooch pin or safety pin onto the back.

Knit Two

Knitted flowers can be used to add a beautifully feminine detail to an accessory. Use them alone as a corsage or a brooch, or add them to a hat for a flirty finish. Several ways of making flowers are detailed below.

For a spiky flower

With your chosen yarn and using needles two sizes smaller than those recommended on the ball band, cast on 5 sts.

Foundation Row K1, yo, k2 and turn.
Row 1 P4.
Row 2 K1, yo, k5.
Row 3 P7.
Row 4 K1, yo, k4 and turn.
Row 5 P6.
Row 6 K1, yo, k7.
Row 7 P9.
Row 8 K1, yo, k6 and turn.
Row 9 P8.
Row 10 K1, yo, k9.
Row 11 P11.
Row 12 Bind off 6 sts, k1 (last st used in binding off), yo, k2 and turn.
Rep these 12 rows 4 times more.
Work rows 1 to 7.
Row 8 Bind off 4 sts, k1, yo, k2 and turn.
Rep these 8 rows 4 times more.
Work rows 1 to 3.
Row 4 Bind off 2 sts, k1 (last st used in binding off), yo, k2.

Rep these 4 rows 3 times more then rows 1 to 3 again.
Bind off.

Run a gathering thread around the base of the flower. Pull up and arrange the three sets of petals into three layers. Work a few stitches through all layers to secure. Sew a button into the centre. Sew on a brooch pin.

For a double flower

With your chosen yarn, use needles two sizes smaller than those recommended on the ball band.

Make the outer ring by working 6 petals as given for the corsage.

To make the inner ring of small petals (make 6):
Cast on 3 sts and knit 1 row.
Work rows 1 to 5 as given for the corsage. 9 sts.
Knit 5 rows.
Work from row 19 to the end.

Make up both rings of petals as given for the corsage. Sew the inner ring of small petals into the outer ring. You could use a different colour or contrasting yarn for the centre petals. Fill the centre with beads, sequins or buttons, or add another layer of even smaller petals by working rows 1 to 3 (7 sts), knitting 5 rows and then working from row 23 to the end. Make a fuller single flower by working a ring of more than six petals.

For a fringed corsage

This flower is fulled, so use a 100% wool yarn to make it.

Use your chosen yarn and needles the size recommended on the ball band. Cast on four times the number of stitches per 4in (10cm) as stated on the ball band. Work 4in (10cm) in st st. Bind off.

Full the knitting. Immerse in hot water (use gloves to protect your hands). Rub with olive oil soap and knead without pulling, stretching or rubbing, to mesh the fibres together. Rinse in cold water, squeeze out excess water, roll in a towel to soak up the remaining water, and dry flat.

Make even cuts about ½in (1cm) apart from one edge to within ¼in (1.5cm) of the opposite edge. Run a gathering thread through the base of the fabric and pull up into gathers. Form the flower by twisting it round and round from the centre. Work a few stitches through all layers to secure. Sew a button or a bead cluster in the centre.

Cable stitch wristwarmers

Wristwarmers are a great way to keep your hands warm while still being able to use your fingers – for knitting, of course! These practical and stylish wristwarmers are made special by the textured cable-panel detail. Cables are fun to make (they're easier than they look) and show up crisply when worked in this smooth yarn. A wool and cashmere mix medium-weight (aran) yarn was chosen for softness and warmth. The wristwarmers are worked in a k2, p2 rib for a snug fit and feature a simple cable panel on the back of each hand. All the instructions you need to knit the cable panel with confidence are supplied overleaf.

yarn

2 x 1¾oz (50g) balls of medium-weight (aran) wool/cashmere mix yarn (98yd/90m per ball) in dark purple

needles

• 1 pair of size 6 (4mm) needles
• cable needle

size

6½in (16.5cm) circumference (unstretched) by 6½in (16.5cm) long. Will stretch to fit palm circumference of up to 9in (23cm)

gauge

36 sts and 27 rows to 4in (10cm) measured over unstretched k2, p2 rib using size 6 (4mm) needles

SPECIAL ABBREVIATIONS

C4F Slip next 2 sts onto a cable needle at front of work, k2, k2 from cable needle

C4B Slip next 2 sts onto a cable needle at back of work, k2, k2 from cable needle

Cr3L Slip next 2 sts onto a cable needle at front of work, p1, k2 from cable needle

Cr3R Slip next st onto a cable needle at back of work, k2, p1 from cable needle

knit note

The panel is worked using C4F and C4B to twist the cables and Cr3L and Cr3R to move the ropes across the fabric (see Cables, *Basics*, page 27). The thumb gusset is increased out of the hand by M1 (see Increasing Stitches, *Basics*, page 23)

Knitting the cable panel: Throughout the project pattern you will refer back to these instructions for knitting the cable panel:

CABLE PANEL (12 STS)
Row 1 K2, p2, C4F, p2, k2.
Row 2 P2, k2, p4, k2, p2.
Row 3 K2, p2, k4, p2, k2.
Row 4 As row 2.
Row 5 As row 1.
Row 6 As row 2.
Row 7 (Cr3L, Cr3R) twice.
Row 8 K1, p4, k2, p4, k1.
Row 9 P1, C4B, p2, C4B, p1.
Row 10 As row 8.
Row 11 (Cr3R, Cr3L) twice.
Row 12 P2, k2, p4, k2, p2.

TIP
Choose an understated colour such as this rich purple to show off the cable details to their best.

Knit your right wristwarmer

Using size 6 (4mm) needles, cast on 52 sts loosely.

Foundation Row 1 (K2, p2) 3 times, k4, (P2, k2) 9 times.

Foundation Row 2 (P2, k2) 9 times, p4, (k2, p2) 3 times.

Commence cable panel.

Row 1 RS (K2, p2) twice, work row 1 of cable panel, (p2, k2) 8 times.

Row 2 (P2, k2) 8 times, work row 2 of cable panel, (k2, p2) twice.

Row 3 (K2, p2) twice, work row 3 of cable panel, (p2, k2) 8 times.

Row 4 (P2, k2) 8 times, work row 4 of cable panel, (k2, p2) twice.

These 4 rows form rib and set cable panel.

Beg with row 5 of cable panel, patt 22 more rows, ending with row 10 of cable panel.

Shape thumb gusset

The thumb on each hand is not added onto the side but more towards the palm. If you hold your hand out straight, palm up, you will see that your thumb naturally falls onto your palm rather than sticking out at the side. Stitches have to be added to accommodate the thumb; this is the thumb gusset. These stitches are made by working a M1 on each side of two stitches. On the thumb gusset, work a M1 twisted to the right as the first increase, and a M1 twisted to the left as the second one.

Keeping cable panel correct

Next Row Patt 26 sts, M1, k2, M1, patt to end. 54 sts.

Next Row Patt 24 sts, p4, patt to end.

Next Row Patt 26 sts, k1, M1, k2, M1, k1, patt to end. 56 sts.

Next Row Patt 24 sts, p6, patt to end.

Next Row Patt 26 sts, k1, M1, k4, M1, k1, patt to end. 58 sts.

Next Row Patt 24 sts, p8, patt to end.

Next Row Patt 26 sts, k1, M1, k6, M1, k1, patt to end. 60 sts.

Next Row Patt 24 sts, p10, patt to end.

Next Row Patt 26 sts, k1, M1, k8, M1, k1, patt to end. 62 sts.

Next Row Patt 24 sts, p12, patt to end.

Thumb

Next Row Patt 26 sts, k12 and turn.

Next Row Cast on 2 sts (using cable method, see Casting On, *Basics*, page 17), p14 (including 2 sts just cast on), turn and cast on 2 sts.

Work 7 rows in st st (1 row k, 1 row p) on these 16 sts only for thumb.

Knit 1 row.

Bind off loosely.

Join thumb seam.

With RS of work facing and using size 6 (4mm) needles, pick up and k 2 sts across base of thumb, patt across 24 unworked sts on left-hand needle. 52 sts.

Cont in patt until work measures approx 6½in (16.5cm), ending with row 6 of cable panel.

Bind off in patt.

Knit your left wristwarmer

Using size 6 (4mm) needles, cast on 52 sts loosely.

Foundation Row 1 (K2, p2) 9 times, k4, (P2, k2) 3 times.

Foundation Row 2 (P2, k2) 3 times, p4, (k2, p2) 9 times.

Commence cable panel.

Row 1 RS (K2, p2) 8 times, work row 1 of cable panel, (p2, k2) twice.

Row 2 (P2, k2) twice, work row 2 of cable panel, (k2, p2) 8 times.

Row 3 (K2, p2) 8 times, work row 3 of cable panel, (p2, k2) twice.

Row 4 (P2, k2) twice, work row 4 of cable panel, (k2, p2) 8 times.

These 4 rows form rib and set cable panel.

Beg with row 5 of cable panel, patt 22 more rows, ending with row 10 of cable panel.

Shape thumb gusset

Keeping cable panel correct

Next Row Patt 24 sts, M1, k2, M1, patt to end. 54 sts.

Next Row Patt 26 sts, p4, patt to end.

Next Row Patt 24 sts, k1, M1, k2, M1, k1, patt to end. 56 sts.

Next Row Patt 26 sts, p6, patt to end.

Next Row Patt 24 sts, k1, M1, k4, M1, k1, patt to end. 58 sts.

Next Row Patt 26 sts, p8, patt to end.

Next Row Patt 24 sts, k1, M1, k6, M1, k1, patt to end. 60 sts.

Next Row Patt 26 sts, p10, patt to end.

Next Row Patt 24 sts, k1, M1, k8, M1, k1, patt to end. 62 sts.

Next Row Patt 26 sts, p12, patt to end.

Thumb

Next Row Patt 24 sts, k12 and turn.

Next Row Cast on 2 sts (using cable cast-on), p14 (including 2 sts just cast on), turn and cast on 2 sts.

Work 8 rows in st st (1 row k, 1 row p) on these 16 sts only for thumb.

Knit 1 row.

Bind off loosely.

Join thumb seam.

With RS of work facing and using size 6 (4mm) needles, pick up and k 2 sts across base of thumb, patt across 26 unworked sts on left-hand needle. 52 sts.

Cont in patt until work measures approx 6½in (16.5cm), ending with row 6 of cable panel.

Bind off in patt.

Making up

Sew in all ends. Join side seams.

TIP

When rejoining the yarn to pick up stitches, leave a long end for sewing in securely as these joins are put under strain; you can also use these ends to sew up any holes that might appear around the thumb base.

Knit Two

For a more subtle effect for the cable panel use a multi-coloured yarn. This is a fabulous single-ply handspun yarn in a range of colours – greens, browns, russets, pale pinks and maroons. The yarn has thick and thin sections so the stitches are uneven and the overall look softer.

TIP
You can simply leave out the thumbs on the pattern. Thumb-less wristwarmers are ideal for wearing over a pair of gloves for extra warmth.

This alternative swatch uses a medium-weight (aran) handspun multi-coloured wool yarn (100% wool – 137yd/126m per ball) in cream, green and brown

Abbreviations

Abbreviations are used in knitting patterns to shorten commonly used terms so that the instructions are easier to read and a manageable length. The following is a list of all the abbreviations you need to make the projects featured in your *How to Knit* box set and many of these are further explained later in this book. The green tinted box opposite lists the most common differences in US and UK knitting terms.

alt	alternate
approx	approximately
beg	beginning
C4B	cable 4 back
C4F	cable 4 front
Cr3L	cross 3 left
Cr3R	cross 3 right
cm	centimetre(s)
cont	continue
dec(s)	decrease/decreasing
DK	double knitting
dpn	double-pointed needles
foll	following
g	gram(s)
g st	garter stitch (k every row)
inc	increase(s)/increasing
in(s)	inch(es)
k	knit
k2tog	knit 2 stitches together (1 stitch decreased)
k3tog	knit 3 stitches together (2 stitches decreased)
k2togtbl	knit 2 stitches together through back of loops (1 stitch decreased)
kf&b	knit into front and back of stitch (increase 1 stitch)
m	metre(s)
mm	millimetres
M1	make one (increase 1 stitch)
oz	ounces
p	purl

US TERM	UK TERM
stockinette stitch	stocking stitch
reverse stockinette stitch	reverse stocking stitch
seed stitch	moss stitch
moss stitch	double moss stitch
bind off	cast off
gauge	tension

patt(s)	pattern(s)
PB	place bead
p2tog	purl 2 stitches together (1 stitch decreased)
p3tog	purl 3 stitches together (2 stitches decreased)
rem	remain/ing
rep(s)	repeat(s)
RS	right side
sk2po	slip 1 stitch, knit 2 stitches together, pass slipped stitch over (decrease 2 stitches)
sl	slip
sl2tog-k1-psso	slip 2 stitches together, knit 1 stitch, pass 2 slipped stitches over (2 stitches decreased)
ssk	slip 2 stitches one at a time, knit 2 slipped stitches together (1 stitch decreased)
st st	stockinette (stocking) stitch
st(s)	stitch(es)
tbl	through back of loop
tog	together
WS	wrong side
wyib	with yarn in back
wyif	with yarn in front
yd(s)	yards(s)
yo	yarn over
*	repeat directions following * as many times as indicated or end of row
[ ]	instructions in square brackets refer to larger sizes
( )	repeat instructions in round brackets the number of times

Yarn Details

Below are listed the specific yarns that were used for the projects in this book, should you wish to recreate them exactly as we have. Yarn companies frequently discontinue colours or yarns, and replace them with new yarns. Therefore, you may find that some of the yarns or colours below are no longer available. However, by referring to the yarn descriptions on the project pages, you will have no trouble finding a substitute.

Substituting yarns

To work out how much replacement yarn you need follow these simple steps. Use it for each colour or yarn used in the project.

1 The number of balls of the recommended yarn x the number of yards/metres per ball = A

2 The number of yards/metres per ball of the replacement yarn = B

3 A ÷ B = number of balls of replacement yarn.

Novelty knit bag

2 x 1¾oz (50g) balls of Twilleys Goldfingering (80% viscose, 20% metalized polyester – 218yd/200m per ball in shade 38 (Red)

Textured stitch throw

11 x 1¾oz (50g) balls of Rowan Denim (100% cotton – 102yd/93m per ball) in shade 229

9 x 1¾oz (50g) balls of Rowan Denim (100% cotton – 102yd/93m per ball) in shade 231

4 x 1¾oz (50g) ball of Twilleys Denim Freedom (100% cotton – 102yd/93m per ball) in shade 102

2 x 1¾oz (50g) ball of Twilleys Denim Freedom (100% cotton – 102yd/93m per ball) in each of shades 103 and 104

4 x 1¾oz (50g) ball of Twilleys Denim Freedom (100% cotton – 102yd/93m per ball) in shade 102

5 x 1¾oz (50g) ball of Elle True Blue Denim (100% cotton – 118yd/108m per ball) in shade 111

2 x 1¾oz (50g) ball of Elle True Blue Denim (100% cotton – 118yd/108m per ball) in shade 112

Seed stitch set

Scarf: 3 x 1¾oz (50g) balls of Rowan Classic Yarns Cashsoft DK (57% wool/33% microfibre/10% cashmere – 142yd/130m per ball) in colour 521

Beret: 2 × 1¾oz (50g) balls of Rowan Classic Yarns Cashsoft DK (57% wool/33% microfibre/10% cashmere – 142yd/130m per ball) in colour 521

Corsage: 1 × 1¾oz (50g) ball of Rowan Classic Yarns Cashsoft DK (57% wool/33% microfibre/10% cashmere – 142yd/130m per ball) in colour 521

Cable stitch wristwarmers

Main Project: 2 × 1¾oz (50g) balls of Debbie Bliss Cashmerino Aran (55% wool/33% microfibre/12% cashmere – 98yd/90m per ball) in colour 607

Swatch: Debbie Bliss Maya (100% wool – 137yd/126m per 3½oz/100g ball) in colour 07

suppliers

Use the contact details listed below to help you to source the yarns and embellishments used for the projects in this book.

Debbie Bliss
www.debbieblissonline.com

(USA)
www.knittingfever.com

(UK)
www.designeryarns.uk.com

(AUS)
www.prestigeyarns.com

Rowan
www.knitrowan.com

Rowan Classic Yarns
www.ryclassic.com

Twilleys
www.twilleysofstamford.co.uk

Other Books

For more about the following titles and other great knitting
books from David & Charles visit: **www.rucraft.co.uk**

Knitter's Bible: Knitted Accessories

A collection of over 30 stylish knitted accessories
for all seasons, from gloves and scarves, to hats and
ponchos. Easy-to-follow techniques ensure great
results for every project.

Knitter's Bible: Knitted Throws & Cushions

An inspiring selection of knitted projects to
brighten up your home, from luxury afghans and
bedspreads to functional cushions and seating.

Knitter's Bible: Knitted Bags

Featuring over 25 gorgeous knitted bags for
every occasion, from cool and casual to smart
and stylish. Uses many of the exciting yarns now
available for modern knitters.

Two Balls or Less

Discover how a little yarn can go a long way with
20 irresistible quick-to-stitch knitting and crochet
projects, each requiring only two balls of yarn, or
less, to complete.

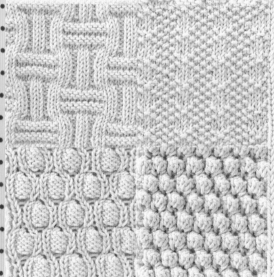

How To Knit: Stitches

Introduction	2
KNIT & PURL STITCHES	4
TEXTURE STITCHES	22
RIB STITCHES	35
Abbreviations	40

A DAVID & CHARLES BOOK
Copyright © David & Charles Limited 2010

Illustrations and photography copyright
© David & Charles Limited 2010
Text copyright © Claire Crompton

Introduction

This book features 38 stitches to help you to explore your new knitting skills. They are presented in three sections: Knit & Purl Stitches, Texture Stitches and Rib Stitches.

Knit & Purl Stitches shows the great variety of fabrics that can be made simply by working knit and purl stitches, and are ideal for the beginner knitter. The section starts with moss stitch, and moves on to basketweave and check patterns, and ends with stars and hearts.

Texture Stitches will help you to turn your knitting three-dimensional. Discover such treats as bubble pattern and gooseberry stitch, as well as ruching and smocking stitches. The final section, Rib Stitches, presents lace ribs as well as ribs suitable for aran sweaters, as well as the wonderful brioche stitch that produces a thick, cosy fabric.

STITCH CHARTS

Many of the knitting patterns featured in the *Stitches* book include a stitch chart. These are designed to assist in the working of the stitches and are an additional visual aid to the pattern instructions included. On the stitch chart each stitch is represented by a symbol, which usually reflects the texture of a stitch. The key for working these charts is as follows, but where additional stitches are required, a key is provided alongside the stitch chart.

KEY

·	p on RS rows, k on WS rows
☐	k on RS rows, p on WS rows

Knit & Purl Stitches

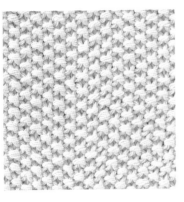

Seed (Moss) Stitch
(reversible)

On an odd number of stitches.
Row 1 K1, * p1, k1; rep from * to end.
Repeat this row.

On an even number of stitches.
Row 1 * K1, p1; rep from * to end.
Row 2 * P1, k1; rep from * to end.
Repeat these 2 rows.

Moss (Double Moss) Stitch
(reversible)

On an odd number of stitches.
Row 1 K1, * p1, k1; rep from * to end.
Row 2 P1, * k1, p1; rep from * to end.
Row 3 As row 2.
Row 4 As row 1.
Repeat these 4 rows.

On an even number of stitches.
Row 1 * K1, p1; rep from * to end.
Row 2 As row 1.
Row 3 * P1, k1; rep from * to end.
Row 4 As row 3.
Repeat these 4 rows.

Moss (Double Moss) Stitch and Rib Check

(reversible)

Multiple of 12 sts plus 7.

Row 1 * (P1, k1) 3 times, p2, (k1, p1) twice; rep from * to last 7 sts, (p1, k1) 3 times, p1.

Row 2 K1, (p1, k1) 3 times, * (k1, p1) twice, k2, (p1, k1) 3 times; rep from * to end.

Row 3 P1, * k1, p1; rep from * to end.

Row 4 K1, * p1, k1; rep from * to end.

Row 5 As row 1.

Row 6 As row 2.

Row 7 * P2, k1, p1, k1, p2, (k1, p1) twice, k1; rep from * to last 7 sts, p2, k1, p1, k1, p2.

Row 8 K2, p1, k1, p1, k2, * (p1, k1) twice, p1, k2, p1, k1, p1, k2; rep from * to end.

Row 9 As row 3.

Row 10 As row 4.

Row 11 As row 7.

Row 12 As row 8.

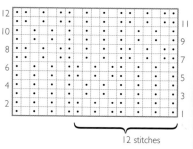

12 stitches

Two Stitch Check
(reversible)

Multiple of 4 sts plus 2.
Row 1 K2, * p2, k2; rep from * to end.
Row 2 P2, * k2, p2; rep from * to end.
Row 3 As row 2.
Row 4 As row 1.
Repeat these 4 rows.

4 stitches

Four Stitch Check
(reversible)

Multiple of 8 sts.
Rows 1, 2, 3 and 4 * K4, p4; rep from * to end.
Rows 5, 6, 7 and 8 * P4, k4; rep from * to end.
Repeat these 8 rows.

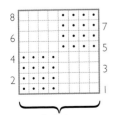

8 stitches

Basketweave

Multiple of 8 sts plus 5.
Row 1 (RS) Knit.
Row 2 * K5, p3; rep from * to last 5 sts, k5.
Row 3 P5, * k3, p5; rep from * to end.
Row 4 As row 2.
Row 5 Knit.
Row 6 K1, p3, k1, * k4, p3, k1; rep from * to end.
Row 7 * P1, k3, p4; rep from * to last 5 sts, p1, k3, p1.
Row 8 As row 6.
Repeat these 8 rows.

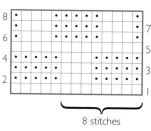

8 stitches

Double Basketweave

Multiple of 18 sts plus 10.
Row 1 (RS) Knit.
Row 2 P10, * p1, k2, p2, k2, p11; rep from * to end.
Row 3 * K1, p8, (k2, p2) twice, k1; rep from * to last 10 sts, k1, p8, k1.
Row 4 P1, k8, p1, * p1, (k2, p2) twice, k8, p1; rep from * to end.
Row 5 * K11, p2, k2, p2, k1; rep from * to last 10 sts, k10.

8

Row 6 As row 2.
Row 7 As row 3.
Row 8 As row 4.
Row 9 As row 5.
Row 10 Purl.
Row 11 * (K2, p2) twice, k10; rep from * to last 10 sts, k2, (p2, k2) twice.
Row 12 P2, (k2, p2) twice, * k8, p2, (k2, p2) twice; rep from * to end.
Row 13 * K2, (p2, k2) twice, p8; rep from * to last 10 sts, k2, (p2, k2) twice.

Row 14 P2, (k2, p2) twice, * p10, (k2, p2) twice; rep from * to end.
Row 15 As row 11.
Row 16 As row 12.
Row 17 As row 13.
Row 18 As row 14.
Repeat these 18 rows.

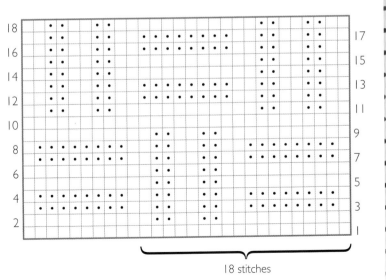

18 stitches

Pennant

Multiple of 7 sts plus 1.
Row 1 (RS) K1, * p1, k6; rep from * to end.
Row 2 * P5, k2; rep from * to last st, p1.
Row 3 K1, * p3, k4; rep from * to end.
Row 4 * P3, k4; rep from * to last st, p1.
Row 5 K1, * p5, k2; rep from * to end.
Row 6 P1, * k6, p1; rep from * to end.
Repeat these 6 rows.

7 stitches

Pyramid

Multiple of 6 sts plus 1.
Row 1 (RS) * K1, p5; rep from * to last st, k1.
Row 2 P1, * k5, p1; rep from * to end.
Row 3 * K2, p3, k1; rep from * to last st, k1.
Row 4 P1, * p1, k3, p2; rep from * to end.
Row 5 * K3, p1, k2; rep from * to last st, k1.
Row 6 P1, * p2, k1, p3; rep from * to end.
Row 7 * P3, k1, p2; rep from * to last st, p1.
Row 8 K1, * k2, p1, k3; rep from * to end.
Row 9 * P2, k3, p1; rep from * to last st, p1.
Row 10 K1, * k1, p3, k2; rep from * to end.
Row 11 * P1, k5; rep from * to last st, p1.
Row 12 K1, * p5, k1; rep from * to end.
Repeat these 12 rows.

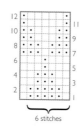

6 stitches

Seed (Moss) Stitch Diamonds

Multiple of 6 sts plus 1.
Row 1 (RS) * K3, p1, k2; rep from * to last st, k1.
Row 2 P1, * (p1, k1) twice, p2; rep from * to end.
Rows 3, 4 and 5 * K1, p1; rep from * to last st, k1.
Row 6 As row 2.
Repeat these 6 rows.

6 stitches

Seed (Moss) Stitch Rib

Multiple of 10 sts plus 1.
Row 1 (RS) * K4, p1, k1, p1, k3; rep from * to last st, k1.

Row 2 P1, * p2, (k1, p3) twice; rep from * to end.
Row 3 * K2, (p1, k1) 4 times; rep from * to last st, k1.
Row 4 P1, * k1, p1, k1, p3, (k1, p1) twice; rep from * to end.
Row 5 As row 3.
Row 6 As row 2.
Repeat these 6 rows.

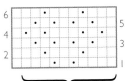

10 stitches

King Charles Brocade

Multiple of 12 sts plus 1.

Row 1 (RS) *K1, p1, k9, p1; rep from * to last st, k1.
Row 2 K1, * p1, k1, p7, k1, p1, k1; rep from * to end.
Row 3 * (K1, p1) twice, k5, p1, k1, p1; rep from * to last st, k1.
Row 4 P1, * (p1, k1) twice, p3, k1, p1, k1, p2; rep from * to end.
Row 5 * K3, p1, (k1, p1) 3 times, k2; rep from * to last st, k1.
Row 6 P1, * p3, k1, (p1, k1) twice, p4; rep from * to end.
Row 7 * K5, p1, k1, p1, k4; rep from * to last st, k1.
Row 8 As row 6.
Row 9 As row 5.
Row 10 As row 4.
Row 11 As row 3.

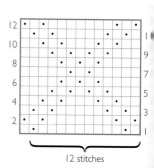

12 stitches

Stepped Diamonds

Multiple of 12 sts plus 2.
Row 1 (RS) * P2, k10; rep from * to last 2 sts, p2.
Row 2 K2, * p10, k2; rep from * to end.
Row 3 * K2, p2, k6, p2; rep from * to last 2 sts, k2.
Row 4 P2, * k2, p6, k2, p2; rep from * to end.
Row 5 * K4, p2, k2, p2, k2; rep from * to last 2 sts, k2.
Row 6 P2, * (p2, k2) twice, p4; rep from * to end.
Row 7 * K6, p2, k4; rep from * to last 2 sts, k2.

Row 8 P2, * p4, k2, p6; rep from * to end.
Row 9 As row 5.
Row 10 As row 6.
Row 11 As row 3.
Row 12 As row 4.
Repeat these 12 rows.

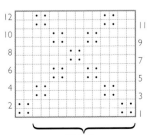

12 stitches

Mock Cable
(reversible)

Multiple of 10 sts.
Row 1 * P4, k1, p1, k4; rep from * to end.
Row 2 *P3, k2, p2, k3; rep from * to end.
Row 3 * P2, k2, p1, k1, p2, k2; rep from * to end.
Row 4 * P1, (k2, p2) twice, k1; rep from * to end.
Row 5 * K2, p3, k3, p2; rep from * to end.
Row 6 * K1, p4, k4, p1; rep from * to end.
Repeat these 6 rows.

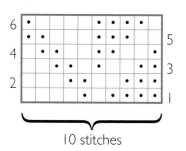

10 stitches

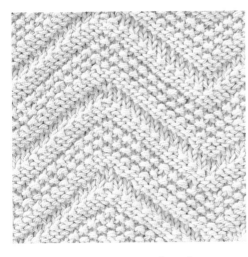

Seed (Moss) Stitch Chevron

Multiple of 22 sts plus 1.
Row 1 (RS) * K1, p3, k1, (p1, k1) twice, p5, k1, (p1, k1) twice, p3; rep from * to last st, k1.
Row 2 P1, * p1, k3, p1, (k1, p1) twice, k3, p1, (k1, p1) twice, k3, p2; rep from * to end.
Row 3 * K3, p3, k1, (p1, k1) 5 times, p3, k2; rep from * to last st, k1.
Row 4 K1, * p3, k3, p1, (k1, p1) 4 times, k3, p3, k1; rep from * to end.
Row 5 * P2, k3, p3, k1, (p1, k1) 3 times, p3, k3, p1; rep from * to last st, p1.
Row 6 K1, * k2, p3, k3, p1, (k1, p1) twice, k3, p3, k3; rep from * to end.
Row 7 * K1, p3, k3, p3, k1, p1, k1, p3, k3, p3; rep from * to last st, k1.

Row 8 K1, * p1, k3, p3, k3, p1, k3, p3, k3, p1, k1; rep from * to end.
Row 9 * K1, p1, k1, p3, k3, p5, k3, p3, k1, p1; rep from * to last st, k1.
Row 10 K1, * p1, k1, p1, (k3, p3) twice, k3, (p1, k1) twice; rep from * to end.
Row 11 * K1, (p1, k1) twice, p3, k3, p1, k3, p3, (k1, p1) twice; rep from * to last st, k1.
Row 12 K1, * p1, (k1, p1) twice, k3, p5, k3, (p1, k1) 3 times; rep from * to end.
Row 13 * P2, k1, (p1, k1) twice, p3, k3, p3, (k1, p1) 3 times; rep from * to last st, p1.
Row 14 K1, * k2, p1, (k1, p1) twice, k3, p1, k3, p1, (k1, p1) twice, k3; rep from * to end.
Repeat these 14 rows.

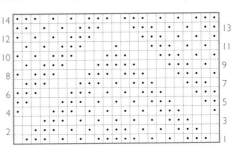

22 stitches

Small Gingham
(reversible)

Multiple of 10 sts plus 5.
Row 1 * P5, k1, (p1, k1) twice; rep from * to last 5 sts, p5.
Row 2 K5, * (k1, p1) twice, k6; rep from * to end.
Rows 3 to 6 Repeat rows 1 and 2 twice more.
Row 7 P1, (k1, p1) twice, * p6, (k1, p1) twice; rep from * to end.
Row 8 * P1, (k1, p1) twice, k5; rep from * to last 5 sts, p1, (k1, p1) twice.
Rows 9 to 12 Repeat rows 7 and 8 twice more.
Repeat these 12 rows.

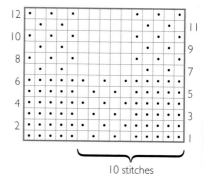

10 stitches

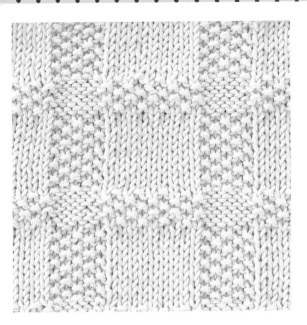

Gingham Check

Multiple of 14 sts plus 9.
Row 1 (RS) * (K1, p1) 4 times, k1, p5; rep from * to last 9 sts, (k1, p1) 4 times, k1.
Row 2 (K1, p1) 4 times, k1, * k6, (p1, k1) 4 times; rep from * to end.
Rows 3 to 5 Repeat rows 1 and 2 once more then row 1 again.
Row 6 P9, * (p1, k1) twice, p10; rep from * to end.
Row 7 * K9, (p1, k1) twice, p1; rep from * to last 9 sts, k9.

Rows 8 to 15 Repeat rows 6 and 7 four times more.
Row 16 As row 6.
Repeat these 16 rows.

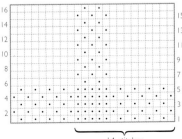

14 stitches

Star in a Square

Multiple of 24 sts plus 1.
Row 1 (RS) * P1, k1; rep from * to last st, p1.
Row 2 Purl.
Row 3 * P1, k23; rep from * to last st, p1.
Row 4 P1, * (p7, k1) twice, p8; rep from * to end.

Row 5 * P1, k8, p1, k5, p1, k8; rep from * to last st, p1.
Row 6 P1, * p7, k1, p1, k1, p3, k1, p1, k1, p8; rep from * to end.
Row 7 * P1, k8, p1, (k1, p1) 3 times, k8; rep from * to last st, p1.
Row 8 P1, * p7, k1, (p1, k1) 4 times, p8; rep from * to end.
Row 9 * P1, k2, p1, (k1, p1) twice, k9, p1, (k1, p1) twice, k2; rep from * to last st, p1.

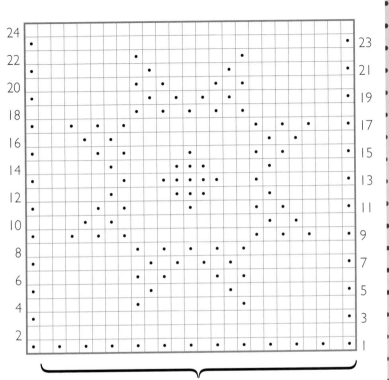

24 stitches

Row 10 P1, * p3, k1, p1, k1, p11, k1, p1, k1, p4; rep from * to end.
Row 11 * P1, k4, p1, k1, (p1, k4) twice, p1, k1, p1, k4; rep from * to last st, p1.
Row 12 P1, * p5, k1, p4, k3, p4, k1, p6; rep from * to end.
Row 13 * P1, k6, p1, k2, p5, k2, p1, k6; rep from * to last st, p1.
Row 14 As row 12

Row 15 As row 11.
Rows 16 to 23 Work from row 10 back to row 3.
Row 24 Purl.
Repeat these 24 rows.

Heart Squares

Multiple of 14 sts plus 1.

Row 1 (RS) * P1, k1; rep from * to last st, p1.

Row 2 Purl.

Row 3 * P1, k6; rep from * to last st, p1.

Row 4 P1, * p5, k3, p6; rep from * to end.

Row 5 * P1, k4, p2, k1, p2, k4; rep from * to last st, p1.

Row 6 P1, * (p3, k2) twice, p4; rep from * to end.

Row 7 * P1, k2, p2, k5, p2, k2; rep from * to last st, p1.

Row 8 P1, * p1, k2, p3, k1, p3, k2, p2; rep from * to end.

Row 9 * P1, k1, p2, k2, p3, k2, p2, k1; rep from * to last st, p1.

Row 10 P1, * p2, k4, p1, k4, p3; rep from * to end.

Row 11 * P1, (k3, p2) twice, k3; rep from * to last st, p1.

Row 12 Purl.

Repeat these 12 rows.

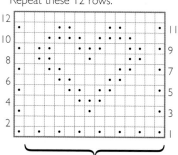

14 stitches

Block Quilting

Multiple of 14 sts.
Row 1 (RS) * K4, p6, k4; rep from * to end.
Row 2 Purl.
Rows 3 and 4 Repeat rows 1 and 2 once more.
Row 5 As row 1.
Row 6 * P3, k2, p4, k2, p3; rep from * to end.
Row 7 * K2, p2, k6, p2, k2; rep from * to end.
Row 8 * P1, k2, p8, k2, p1; rep from * to end.
Row 9 * P2, k10, p2; rep from * to end.
Row 10 As row 8.
Row 11 As row 7.
Row 12 As row 6.
Repeat these 12 rows.

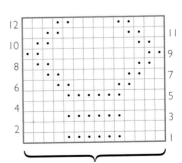

14 stitches

Texture Stitches

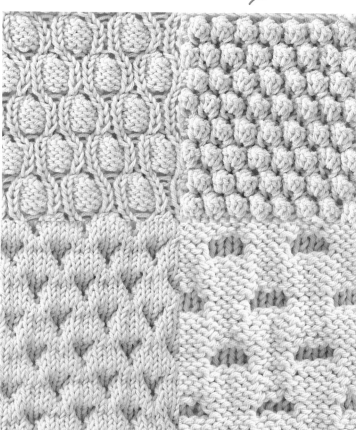

Ruching

On an odd number of stitches.
Row 1 (RS) Knit.
Row 2 Purl.
Rows 3 and 4 Repeat rows 1 and 2 once more.
Row 5 K1, * k into front and back of next st, k1; rep from * to end.
Row 6 Knit.
Row 7 Purl.
Rows 8 to 12 Repeat rows 6 and 7 twice more, then row 6 again.
Row 13 P1, * p2tog, p1; rep from * to end.
Row 14 Knit.
Repeat these 14 rows.

Bubble Pattern

Multiple of 10 sts plus 2.
Row 1 (RS) Knit.
Row 2 Purl.
Row 3 K1, * (k5, turn, p5, turn) 3 times, k10; rep from * to end, ending last rep with k1.
Row 4 Purl.
Row 5 Knit.
Row 6 Purl.
Row 7 K6, * (k5, turn, p5, turn) 3 times, k10; rep from * to last st, k1.
Row 8 Purl.
Repeat these 8 rows.

Cocoon Stitch

Abbreviation:
M5 – (p1, yo, p1, yo, p1) all into next st.

Multiple of 8 sts plus 7.
Row 1 (RS) * K1, p5, k1, p1; rep from * to last 7 sts, k1, p5, k1.
Row 2 P1, sl 2 wyif, p3tog, psso, p1, * M5, p1, sl 2 wyif, p3tog, psso, p1; rep from * to end.
Rows 3, 5 and 7 * K1, p1, k1, p5; rep from * to last 3 sts, k1, p1, k1.
Rows 4 and 6 P1, k1, p1, * k5, p1, k1, p1; rep

from * to end.
Row 8 P1, M5, p1, * sl 2 wyif, p3tog, psso, p1, M5, p1; rep from * to end.
Row 9 As row 1.
Row 10 P1, k5, p1, * k1, p1, k5, p1; rep from * to end.

Row 11 As row 1.
Row 12 As row 10.
Repeat these 12 rows.

KEY

5	p5 on RS rows, k5 on WS rows
↑	sl 2 wyif, p3tog, psso
↓	M5
·	p on RS rows, k on WS rows
□	k on RS rows, p on WS rows

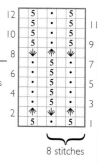

8 stitches

Popcorn Pattern

Abbreviations:

MK – purl next 3 sts then pass 2nd and 3rd sts over first st.

MS – (k1, p1, k1) all into next st.

Multiple of 4 sts plus 3 (stitch count varies).

Row 1 (RS) Knit.

Row 2 P1, MS, p1, * p2, MS, p1; rep from * to end.

Row 3 * K1, MK, k2; rep from * to last 5 sts, k1, MK, k1.

Row 4 Purl.

Row 5 Knit.

Row 6 P3, * MS, p3; rep from * to end.

Row 7 * K3, MK; rep from * to last 3 sts,

Row 8 Purl.

Repeat these 8 rows.

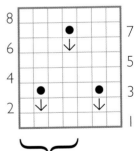

4 stitches

KEY

●	MK
↓	MS
□	k on RS rows, p on WS rows

25

smocking

Abbreviation:

smocking st – insert RH needle from front between 6th and 7th sts, wrap yarn around needle and draw through a loop, sl this loop on to LH needle and k tog with first st on LH needle.

Multiple of 16 sts plus 2.
Row 1 (RS) P2, * k2, p2; rep from * to end.
Row 2 * K2, p2; rep from * to last 2 sts, k2.
Row 3 P2, * smocking st, k1, p2, k2, p2; rep from * to end.
Rows 4 and 6 As row 2.
Row 5 As row 1.
Row 7 P2, k2, p2, * smocking st, k1, p2, k2, p2; rep from * to last 4 sts, k2, p2.
Row 8 As row 2.
Repeat these 8 rows.

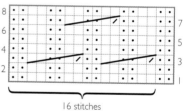

16 stitches

KEY

·	p on RS rows, k on WS rows
□	k on RS rows, p on WS rows
╱	k2tog

— smocking stitch

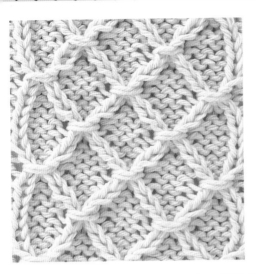

Smocked Honeycomb

Abbreviation:

tie st – sl next 5 sts on to cable needle, wrap yarn around these 5 sts twice, then k1, p3, k1 from cable needle.

Multiple of 16 sts plus 3.
Row 1 (RS) P3, * k1, p3; rep from * to end.
Row 2 * K3, p1; rep from * to last 3 sts, k3.
Row 3 P3, * tie st, p3; rep from * to end.
Rows 4 and 6 As row 2.
Row 5 As row 1.
Row 7 P3, k1, * p3, tie st; rep from * to end, ending last rep with k1, p3.
Row 8 As row 2.
Repeat these 8 rows.

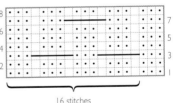

16 stitches

KEY

⊡ p on RS rows, k on WS rows

☐ k on RS rows, p on WS rows

── tie stitch

Boxed Bobble

Abbreviation:
MB – k into front, back and front of
next st and turn, k3 and turn, p3 and
pass 2nd and 3rd sts over first st.

Multiple of 6 sts plus 1.
Row 1 (RS) Purl.
Row 2 and every foll alt row Purl.
Row 3 P1, * k5, p1; rep from * to
end.
Row 5 P1, * k2, MB, k2, p1; rep from
* to end.
Row 7 As row 3.
Row 8 Purl.
Repeat these 8 rows.

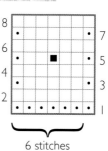

6 stitches

KEY

■	MB
•	p on RS rows, k on WS rows
□	k on RS rows, p on WS rows

Gooseberry Stitch

Abbreviation:
M5 – (p1, yo, p1, yo, p1) all into next st.

Multiple of 4 sts plus 1.
Row 1 (RS) Knit.
Row 2 K1, * M5, k1; rep from * to end.
Row 3 Purl.
Row 4 K1, * sl 2 wyif, p3tog, psso, k1; rep from * to end.
Row 5 Knit.
Row 6 K1, * k1, M5, k1; rep from * to last st, k1.
Row 7 Purl.
Row 8 K1, * k1, sl 2 wyif, p3tog, psso, k1; rep from * to last st, k1.
Repeat these 8 rows.

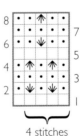

4 stitches

KEY

↑	sl 2 wyif, p3tog, psso
↓	M5
·	p on RS rows, k on WS rows
☐	k on RS rows, p on WS rows

Bobble Circle Pattern

Abbreviation:
MS – (k1, p1, k1) all into next st.

Multiple of 12 sts plus 3.
Row 1 (RS) Knit.
Row 2 * P6, MS, p1, MS, p3; rep from * to last 3 sts, p3.
Row 3 K3, * k3, p3, k1, p3, k6; rep from * to end.
Row 4 * P4, MS, (p1, p3tog) twice, p1, MS, p1; rep from * to last 3 sts, p3.
Row 5 K3, * k1, p3, k5, p3, k4; rep from * to end.
Row 6 * P3, MS, p3tog, p5, p3tog, MS; rep from * to last 3 sts, p3.
Row 7 K3, * p3, k7, p3, k3; rep from * to end.
Row 8 * P3, p3tog, p7, p3tog; rep from * to last 3 sts, p3.
Row 9 Knit.
Row 10 * P3, MS, p7, MS; rep from * to last 3 sts, p3.

Row 11 As row 7.
Row 12 * P3, p3tog, MS, p5, MS, p3tog; rep from * to last 3 sts, p3.
Row 13 As row 5.
Row 14 * P4, p3tog, (p1, MS) twice, p1, p3tog, p1; rep from * to last 3 sts, p3.
Row 15 As row 3.
Row 16 * P6, p3tog, p1, p3tog, p3; rep from * to last 3 sts, p3.
Row 17 Knit.
Row 18 Purl.
Repeat these 18 rows.

KEY

↑ 3 ↓	p3tog
3	p3
↓	MS
☐	k on RS rows, p on WS rows

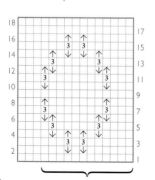

12 stitches

30

Dimple Stitch

Abbreviation:

gathering st – take yarn to back of work as though to knit, insert needle from below under 3 strands, k the next st, bring the st out under the strands.

Multiple of 6 sts plus 5.
Row 1 (RS) Knit.
Row 2 P1, * sl 3 wyif, p3; rep from * to end, ending last rep with p1.
Row 3 K1, * sl 3 wyib, k3; rep from * to end, ending last rep with k1.
Row 4 As row 2.
Rows 5 and 7 Knit.
Row 6 Purl.
Row 8 P2, * gathering st, p5; rep from * to end, ending last rep with p2.
Row 9 Knit.
Row 10 P1, * p3, sl 3 wyif; rep from * to last 4 sts, p4.

Row 11 K4, * sl 3 wyif, k3; rep from * to last st, k1.
Row 12 As row 10.
Rows 13 and 15 Knit.
Row 14 Purl.
Row 16 P5, * gathering st, p5; rep from * to end.
Repeat these 16 rows.

KEY

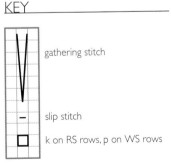

gathering stitch

— slip stitch

☐ k on RS rows, p on WS rows

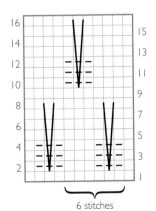

6 stitches

Bramble Stitch

Abbreviation:
MS – (k1, p1, k1) all into next st.

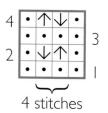

4 stitches

Multiple of 4 sts plus 2.
Row 1 (RS) Purl.
Row 2 K1, * MS, p3tog; rep from * to last st, k1.
Row 3 Purl.
Row 4 K1, * p3tog, MS; rep from * to last st, k1.
Repeat these 4 rows.

KEY

↑	p3tog
↓	MS
·	p on RS rows, k on WS rows

32

Blind Buttonhole Stitch

Multiple of 8 sts plus 6.
Row 1 (WS) Knit.
Row 2 Purl.
Rep these 2 rows once more then row 1 again.
Row 6 K1, * sl 4 wyib, k4; rep from * to last 5 sts, sl 4 wyib, k1.
Row 7 P1, sl 4 wyif, * p4, sl 4 wyif; rep from * to last st, p1.
Rep these 2 rows once more then row 6 again.

Row 11 Knit.
Row 12 Purl.
Rep these 2 rows once more then row 11 again.
Row 16 K5, * sl 4 wyib, k4; rep from * to last st, k1.
Row 17 P5, * sl 4 wyif, p4; rep from * to last st, p1.
Rep these 2 rows once more.
Row 20 As row 16.
Repeat these 20 rows.

Rib Stitches

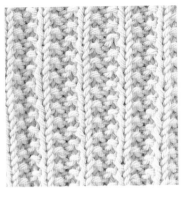

Mistake Rib

Multiple of 4 sts plus 3.
Row 1 * K2, p2; rep from * to last 3 sts, k2, p1.
Repeat this row.

4 stitches

Brioche Stitch

Even number of sts.
Foundation row * Yo, sl 1 wyib, k1; rep from * to end.
Row 1 * Yo, sl 1 wyib, k2tog (sl st and yo of previous row); rep from * to end.
Repeat row 1.

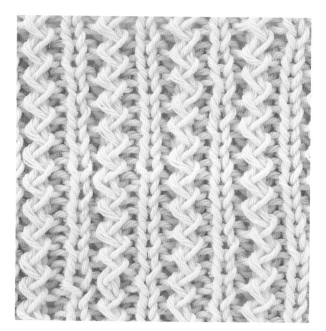

Rick Rack Rib

Abbreviations:
twist k – take RH needle behind first st and k into back of second st, k first st, slip both sts off LH needle.
twist p – with yarn in front, miss first st and p into second st, p first st, sl both sts off LH needle together.

Multiple of 5 sts plus 1.
Row 1 (RS) K1, * p1, twist k, p1, k1; rep from * to end.
Row 2 * P1, k1, twist p, k1; rep from * to last st, p1.
Repeat these 2 rows.

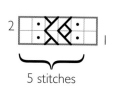

5 stitches

KEY

✕✕	twist k
⅄⋋	twist p
·	p on RS rows, k on WS rows
□	k on RS rows, p on WS rows

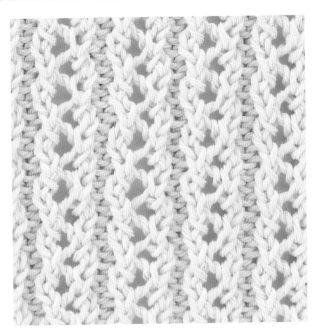

Openwork Rib

Multiple of 5 sts plus 2.
Row 1 (RS) P2, * k1, yo, ssk, p2; rep from * to end.
Row 2 * K2, p3; rep from * to last 2 sts, k2.
Row 3 P2, * k2tog, yo, k1, p2; rep from * to end.
Row 4 As row 2.
Repeat these 4 rows.

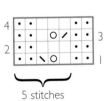

5 stitches

KEY

O	yo
/	k2tog
\	ssk
·	p on RS rows, k on WS rows
☐	k on RS rows, p on WS rows

Aran Rib 1

Abbreviation:
Cr3L – slip 1 st on to cable needle
at front, k1 tbl, p1, then k1 tbl from
cable needle.

Multiple of 8 sts plus 3.
Row 1 (RS) * K3, (p1, k1 tbl) twice,
p1; rep from * to last 3 sts, k3.
Row 2 P3, * (k1, p1 tbl) twice, k1;
rep from * to end.
Row 3 * K3, p1, Cr3L, p1; rep from *
to last 3 sts, k3.
Row 5 As row 1.
Row 6 As row 2.
Repeat these 6 rows.

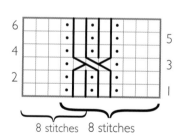

8 stitches   8 stitches

KEY
_____

Cr3L

p on RS rows, k on WS rows
k on RS rows, p on WS rows

Aran Rib 2

Abbreviations:

Cr2L – slip 1 st on to cable needle at front, p1, k1 tbl from cable needle.

Cr2R – slip 1 st on to cable needle at back, k1 tbl, p1 from cable needle.

Multiple of 7 sts plus 4.

Row 1 (RS) * K4, Cr2L, p1; rep from * to last 4 sts, k4.

Row 2 P4, * k1, p1 tbl, k1, p4; rep from * to end.

Row 3 * K4, p1, Cr2L; rep from * to last 4 sts, k4.

Row 4 P4, * p1 tbl, k2, p4; rep from * to end.

Row 5 * K4, p1, Cr2R; rep from * to last 4 sts, k4.

Row 6 As row 2.

Row 7 * K4, Cr2R, p1; rep from * to last 4 sts, k4.

Row 8 P4, * k2, p1 tbl, p4; rep from * to end.

Repeat these 8 rows.

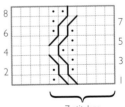

7 stitches

KEY

Cr2R

Cr2L

⊡ p on RS rows, k on WS rows

☐ k on RS rows, p on WS rows

Abbreviations

Abbreviations are used in knitting patterns to shorten commonly used terms so that the instructions are easier to read and a manageable length. The following is a list of all the abbreviations you need to make the projects featured in your *How to Knit* box set and many of these are further explained later in this book. The green tinted box opposite lists the most common differences in US and UK knitting terms.

alt	alternate
approx	approximately
beg	beginning
C4B	cable 4 back
C4F	cable 4 front
Cr3L	cross 3 left
Cr3R	cross 3 right
cm	centimetre(s)
cont	continue
dec(s)	decrease/decreasing
DK	double knitting
dpn	double-pointed needles
foll	following
g	gram(s)
g st	garter stitch (k every row)
inc	increase(s)/increasing
in(s)	inch(es)
k	knit
k2tog	knit 2 stitches together (1 stitch decreased)
k3tog	knit 3 stitches together (2 stitches decreased)
k2togtbl	knit 2 stitches together through back of loops (1 stitch decreased)
kf&b	knit into front and back of stitch (increase 1 stitch)
m	metre(s)
mm	millimetres
M1	make one (increase 1 stitch)
oz	ounces
p	purl

US TERM	UK TERM
stockinette stitch	stocking stitch
reverse stockinette stitch	reverse stocking stitch
seed stitch	moss stitch
moss stitch	double moss stitch
bind off	cast off
gauge	tension

patt(s)	pattern(s)
PB	place bead
p2tog	purl 2 stitches together (1 stitch decreased)
p3tog	purl 3 stitches together (2 stitches decreased)
rem	remain/ing
rep(s)	repeat(s)
RS	right side
sk2po	slip 1 stitch, knit 2 stitches together, pass slipped stitch over (decrease 2 stitches)
sl	slip
sl2tog-k1-psso	slip 2 stitches together, knit 1 stitch, pass 2 slipped stitches over (2 stitches decreased)
ssk	slip 2 stitches one at a time, knit 2 slipped stitches together (1 stitch decreased)
st st	stockinette (stocking) stitch
st(s)	stitch(es)
tbl	through back of loop
tog	together
WS	wrong side
wyib	with yarn in back
wyif	with yarn in front
yd(s)	yards(s)
yo	yarn over
*	repeat directions following * as many times as indicated or end of row
[ ]	instructions in square brackets refer to larger sizes
( )	repeat instructions in round brackets the number of times

Contents

How To Knit:
Embellished Knits

Introduction	2
BALLET SLIPPER BLING	4
KNITTED TRIM CUSHION	12
INTARSIA FLOWER BAG	22
SEQUINNED KNITTED THROW	28
Abbreviations	36
Yarn Details	38
Suppliers	40
Other Books	41

Introduction

Embellished knits can really make your knitted projects stand out from the crowd, and there are lots of different ways to add embellishment and decoration to your knitting. The projects in this book explore a few favourites.

The sweet ballerina-style slippers illustrate perfectly how decorative accents such as floral or button embellishments or simple embroidered motifs can personalize your knits. Knitted roses bloom across a basic knitted cushion for a terrific three-dimensional decoration, and a summery bag shows how you can work a floral motif as you knit with the intarsia technique. Finally, bring a touch of luxury to a simple throw by knitting in sequins as you go.

Also squeezed in are extra ideas for varying the patterns included so look out for the Knit Twos, Threes or even more. For the specific yarn details for all of the projects featured in this book, see pages 38–39.

3

Ballet slipper bling

These lovely slippers are made in simple
stockinette stitch in a hard-wearing acrylic yarn
that can be washed in the machine. You can dress
them up however you like; the slippers shown
here are embellished with a vivid yellow artificial
flower that contrasts boldly with the hot pink.
Modelled on the classic, elegant shape of ballet
shoes, they're perfect for blissing out in your
boudoir, or just hanging out at home. Make the
slippers in vibrant colours and experiment with
embellishments – beads, buttons, sequins and
embroidery. There are many ways to make your
ballet shoes beautiful – just turn to page 10 for
more ideas.

yarn
1 × 3½oz (100g) ball of light-weight
(DK) acrylic yarn in bright pink

needles and notions
- 1 pair of size 6 (4mm) needles
- 1 size G6 (4.00mm) crochet hook
- Artificial flower petals
- Contrasting bead for centre of flower

size
Small [Medium: Large]

gauge
22 sts and 30 rows to 4in (10cm)
square measured over st st using size
6 (4mm) needles

knit note
The crochet instructions are given
in US terms with the UK translation
given in brackets

TIP
*For a more luxurious feel,
make these slippers in a
light-weight (DK) yarn.*

Knit your slippers (make 2)

Sole

Using size 6 (4mm) needles, cast on 12 [12: 14] sts
Row 1 K.
Row 2 P1, pfb, k8 [8: 10], pfb, p1. 14 [14: 16] sts.
Row 3 K.
Row 4 P1, pfb, k10 [10: 12], pfb, p1. 16 [16: 18] sts.
Row 5 K.
Row 6 P1, pfb, k12 [12: 14], pfb, p1. 18 [18: 20] sts.**
Work 53 [55: 57] rows in st st.
Next row P1, p2tog, k10 [12: 14], p2tog tbl, p1. 16 [16: 18] sts.
Next row K.
Next row P1, p2tog, k8 [10: 12], p2tog tbl, p1. 14 [14: 16] sts.
Next row K.
Next row P1, p2tog, k6 [8: 10], p2tog tbl, p1. 12 [12: 14] sts.
Next row K.
Bind off.

Top of slipper

Work as for sole to **.
Work 18 rows in st st.
Next row K8 [8: 9] sts, bind off 2 sts, k8 [8: 9] sts. 16 [16: 18] sts.
Next row Working on first 8 [8: 9] sts only, p.
Next row K2tog tbl, k to end. 7 [7: 8] sts.
Next row P.
Next row K2tog tbl, k to end. 6 [6: 7] sts.
Next row P.
Work 10 [10: 12] rows in st st ending on P row.
Next row K1, m1, k5 [5: 6] sts. 7 [7: 8] sts.
Work 7 rows in st st.
Next row K1, m1, k6 [6: 7] sts. 8 [8: 9] sts.
Work 9 rows in st st.
Next row K1, m1, k7 [7: 8] sts. 9 [9: 10] sts.
Next row P.
Bind off.
Rejoin yarn to rem sts and rep for other side, reversing shapings.

Making up

With right sides facing, join sole to top of foot, and then seam the two sides of the heel together, using mattress stitch (see Finishing Techniques, *Basics*, page 36).

Crochet edging

With size G6 (4mm) crochet hook, work a round of sc (US: single crochet/UK: double crochet) in a number divisible by 4.

Next round Chain 1, work 2 sc into next 2 sts, *miss 1 st, work 3 sc, rep from * to end. Fasten off.

Double strap.

Add the petals of an artificial flower to the slipper and secure in place with a contrasting bead.

Adding a strap

If you wish, you can add a knitted strap to help to keep the slippers on your feet.

Using size 6 (4mm) needles, cast on 3 sts.

Work in garter st (every row knit) until strap measures 5in (12.5cm). Bind off.

Single strap.

Using the photograph on page 11 as a guide, attach one side of the strap(s) to the inside of the slipper where the crochet edge meets the knitting edge. Attach the other end to the outside of the slipper on the other side. Finish by sewing a button onto the end of the strap.

Double crossover strap.

These slippers are knitted flat on straight needles and then the two sides of the heel are seamed together.

The slippers are finished off with a crocheted trim around the opening.

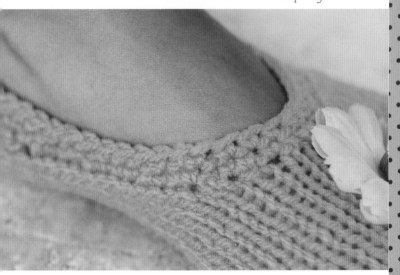

Knit Two

There are many ways to embellish your slippers. Pictured are just three ideas to get you started. For the embroidered slippers, use a contrasting yarn to embroider a spiral pattern. For the button slippers, add some matching buttons in a random pattern using a strong thread, and for the beaded slippers attach beads in the shape of a snowflake. Adding straps also gives a different look, and the variations are endless. See page 8 for instructions.

you will need

yarn
Embroidered slippers: 1 × 3½oz (100g) ball of light-weight (DK) acrylic yarn in yellow
Button slippers: 1 × 3½oz (100g) ball of light-weight (DK) acrylic yarn in turquoise
Beaded slippers: 1 × 3½oz (100g) ball of light-weight (DK) acrylic yarn in purple

Knitted trim cushion

This project shows you how you can take a basic cushion pattern and give it any number of imaginative variations and embellishments through the addition of trimmings. The main project uses a wonderfully smooth wool/silk mix yarn in a deep green for the cushion itself, while the sumptuous rose embellishments are knitted in three colourways of a hand-dyed variegated yarn in silk. The same yarn is used for the leaves, in a shade of green that complements the background green of the cushion. For more ideas on how to embellish the basic cushion, ranging from simply sewing on bought trims to making your own pompoms, see pages 18–20.

you will need

yarn

• **A** 4 × 1¾oz (50g) balls of light-weight (DK) silk/wool yarn (131yd/120m per ball) in dark green

• **B** For roses: 3 × 11yd (10m) skeins of hand-dyed silk thread (equivalent to light-weight/DK yarn) in each of three colourways of pinks/fuchsias/mauves

• **C** For leaves: 2 × 11yd (10m) skeins of hand-dyed silk thread (equivalent to light-weight/DK yarn) in colourway of greens

needles and notions

• 1 pair of size 6 (4mm) needles
• 1 pair of size 7 (4.5mm) needles
• 16in (40cm) cushion pad

size

16in (40cm) square

gauge

22 sts and 28 rows to 4in (10cm) measured over st st (1 row k, 1 row p) using size 6 (4mm) needles

silky dark rose

dark pink wool

lilac cotton

light pink cotton

dark green wool

Knit your cushion

Back and front (make 2 the same)
Using size 6 (4mm) needles and A, cast on 88 sts.
Work in st st (1 row k, 1 row p) until work measures 16in (40cm), ending with a p row.
Bind off.

Roses (make 9)
Using size 7 (4.5mm) needles and B, cast on 80 sts.
Knit 1 row.
Purl 1 row.
Next Row *K2tog; rep from * to end. 40 sts.
Purl 1 row.
Next Row *K2tog; rep from * to end. 20 sts.
Purl 1 row.
Next Row *K2tog; rep from * to end. 10 sts.
Bind off purlwise, leaving a long tail for sewing up.
Curl the rose from the middle with the st st side facing outwards. Secure with a few stitches through all thicknesses on the cast off edge.

Leaves (make 11)
Using size 7 (4.5mm) needles and C, cast on 3 sts.
Purl 1 row.
Next Row (K1, yo) twice, k1. 5 sts.
Purl 1 row.
Next Row k2, yo, k1, yo, k2. 7 sts.
Work 5 rows in st st, beg with a p row.
Next Row Ssk, k3, k2tog. 5 sts.
Purl 1 row.
Next Row Ssk, k1, k2tog. 3 sts.
Purl 1 row.
Next Row Sl2tog, k1, p2sso.
Cut yarn and thread through rem st.

Making up

Sew in all ends on the cushion pieces and press according to instructions on ball bands. Sew roses in a square three roses wide by three roses high in the centre of the front. Sew the leaves around the roses. Join back and front together around three sides. Insert cushion pad and sew remaining side closed.

TIP
If the cushion pad shows through, you may need to cover it with a fabric lining in a colour that matches the knitted fabric.

Make a collection of cushions around a simple colour palette and decorate them in different ways. Buying trims, ribbons and braids is a quick way of finishing; there is a great choice available to suit every taste. Go for bright, funky trims on a hot palette of yarns for a contemporary look, or use darker, richer colours for dramatic interiors. For a more classic effect, choose sugared-almond colours on a palette of soft pastels for a romantic, country look, or a neutral palette with linen, hemp and cotton for a tranquil room. For details of the colours and embellishments shown here, see pages 18–21. All patterns make a 16in (40cm) square cushion.

Knit Two

The yarn used for this boudoir-fabulous cushion is a knitted cord in a great olive green that picks up one of the shades in the funky ostrich-feather trim.

you will need

yarn
5 × 1¾oz (50g) balls of medium-weight (aran) wool/cashmere knitted tube yarn (83yd/75m per ball) in light olive green

needles and notions
• 1 pair of size 7 (4.5mm) needles
• 65in (163cm) of dark olive ostrich trim

gauge
18 sts and 24 rows to 4in (10cm) square measured over st st (1 row k, 1 row p) using size 7 (4.5mm) needles

Knit your cushion

Back and front (make 2 the same)
Using size 7 (4.5mm) needles, cast on 72 sts.
Work in st st (1 row k, 1 row p) until work measures 16in (40cm), ending with a p row.
Bind off.

Making up

Sew in all ends neatly. Press according to instructions on ball bands. Join back and front together around three sides. Insert cushion pad and sew remaining side closed. Sew ostrich-feather trim around the cushion, overlapping ends at one corner.

Knit Three

This elegant cushion is knitted in a textural viscose/silk/linen mix yarn that features multi-coloured threads speckled throughout the fabric. It is decorated with beaded and sequinned trims in complementary shades of green, using a soft velvet ribbon for a luxurious finish.

you will need

yarn
5 x 1¾oz (50g) balls of medium-weight (aran) viscose/silk yarn (71yd/65m per ball) in light yellow-green

needles and notions
• 1 pair of size 7 (4.5mm) needles
• 17in (43cm) lengths of ribbons, sequinned or beaded trims

gauge
18 sts and 24 rows to 4in (10cm) square measured over st st (1 row k, 1 row p) using size 7 (4.5mm) needles

Knit your cushion

Back and front (make 2 the same)
Work as given for the feathered trimmed cushion (Knit Two).

Making up

Sew in all ends neatly. Press according to instructions on ball bands. Sew trims and ribbons onto the front, turning in the raw ends to prevent fraying. Join back and front together around three sides. Insert a cushion pad and sew remaining side closed.

Knit Four

This cuddly, playful pompom cushion is knitted in a smooth wool mix yarn, while the pompoms are made using three contrasting textures. You could use shop-bought pompoms, but it's much more fun to make your own, and you can create exactly the colours and textures you want. For how to make a pompom, see Special Techniques, *Basics*, page 34.

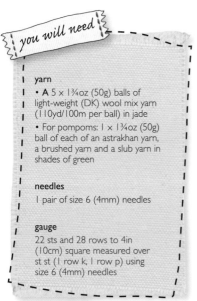

you will need

yarn
• **A** 5 x 1¾oz (50g) balls of light-weight (DK) wool mix yarn (110yd/100m per ball) in jade
• For pompoms: 1 x 1¾oz (50g) ball of each of an astrakhan yarn, a brushed yarn and a slub yarn in shades of green

needles
1 pair of size 6 (4mm) needles

gauge
22 sts and 28 rows to 4in (10cm) square measured over st st (1 row k, 1 row p) using size 6 (4mm) needles

Knit your cushion

Back and front (make 2 the same)
Using size 6 (4mm) needles and A, cast on 88 sts.
Work in st st (1 row k, 1 row p) until work measures 16in (40cm), ending with a p row.
Bind off.

Making up

Sew in all ends neatly. Press according to instructions on ball bands. Using yarn A and the three contrasting yarns, make sufficient pompoms to cover the front of the cushion, using one yarn for a pompom and also mixing two or even three yarns together. Sew onto the front. Join back and front together around three sides. Insert cushion pad and sew remaining side closed.

Intarsia flower bag

This is a great summer bag. The vivid orange flowers are worked using intarsia, while the leaves are knitted separately and sewn on for a three-dimensional touch, and a simple backstitch is used to add extra decorative detail for the flower stems and centres. The bag's stylish flared shape is created by decreasing the sides. Knitted in ever-versatile cotton yarn, this bag is robust enough to take on the beach, and smart and sassy enough to take to garden parties and barbecues. Cotton is available in many vibrant colours; here a hot pink background was chosen to contrast with the zingy orange flowers and the fresh green leaves.

yarn

• **A** 3 × 1¾oz (50g) balls of light-weight (DK) cotton (93yd/85m per ball) in pink

• **B** 1 × 1¾oz (50g) ball of light-weight (DK) cotton (93yd/85m per ball) in orange

• **C** 1 × 1¾oz (50g) ball of light-weight (DK) cotton (93yd/85m per ball) in green

needles and notions

• 1 pair of size 6 (4mm) needles
• 2 bamboo ring handles

size

13in (33cm) at widest point and 11in (28cm) long (excluding handles)

gauge

20 sts and 28 rows to 4in (10cm) measured over st st (1 row k, 1 row p) using size 6 (4mm) needles and A

knit note

Intarsia is the technique of colour knitting using a separate ball or bobbin of colour for each block. For full details, see *Basics*, page 30

TIP
Use yarns with a silk content for a touch of luxury or fluid viscose ribbon yarns for shimmer.

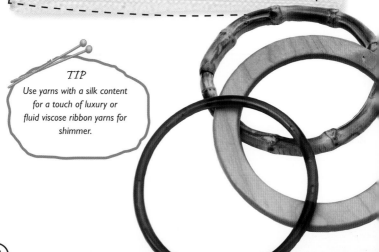

Knit your bag

Front

Using size 6 (4mm) needles and A, cast on 66 sts.

Work 2 rows in st st (1 row k, 1 row p) starting with a k row.

Commence chart

Working RS rows (odd) from right to left and WS rows (even) from left to right, and dec 1 st at each end of 13th and every foll 8th row, work in st st from chart until the 64th row has been completed. 52 sts.

Using A, work 20 rows in st st.

Bind off.

TIP

When changing from one colour to another, twist the yarns together to prevent a hole from appearing.

Back

Using size 6 (4mm) needles and A, cast on 66 sts.

Work in st st, starting with a k row, dec 1 st at each end of 15th and every foll 8th row to 52 sts.

Work 23 rows in st st.

Bind off.

The ready-made bamboo rings are quickly and easily attached and give this bag a stylish finish.

Leaves (make 10)

Using size 6 (4mm) needles and C, cast on 3 sts and p 1 row.

Row 1 RS K1, (yo, k1) twice. 5 sts.

Row 2 and every foll WS row P.

Row 3 K2, yo, k1, yo, k2. 7 sts.

Row 5 K3, yo, k1, yo, k3. 9 sts.

Row 7 Ssk, k5, k2tog. 7 sts.

Row 9 Ssk, k3, k2tog. 5 sts.

Row 11 Ssk, k1, k2tog. 3 sts.

Row 13 Sk2po.

Cut yarn, thread through rem st and pull up tightly.

Making up

Sew in all ends. Press according to instructions on ball bands. On front, sew a pair of leaves next to each flower (use the photographs opposite for reference). Using C and backstitch (see *Basics*, page 34), work a stem between the leaves and flowers and a swirl in the centre of each flower. Using mattress stitch (see *Basics*, page 36) join the base seam, and join the side seams up to penultimate decrease. Pull top edge through one of the handles from front to back and fold over to enclose the handle. Sew turnover neatly in place using a running stitch. Repeat for other handle.

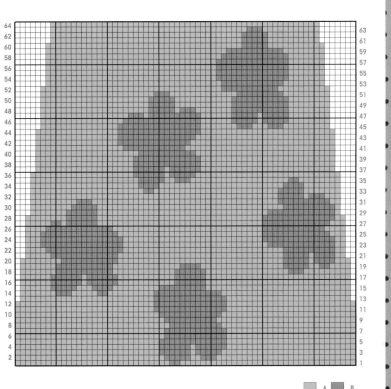

A ▨ B

sequinned knitted throw

You can take a fairly plain knitted fabric and embellish it with shop-bought trimmings. Take this small throw for example: a simple rectangle knitted in stockinette stitch in a beautifully lush medium-weight (aran) wool and silk mix yarn in a deep, rich purple, its true impact comes from the large gold sequins (paillettes) that are knitted in to create a border. The addition of a metallic flecked fringe decorated with both gold and wine-red sequins, is the perfect finishing touch. The throw is an ideal size to drape over a chair and its shimmering sequinned border will reflect the glow of candles on dark winter evenings.

yarn

• **A** 10 x 1¾oz (50g) balls of medium-weight (aran) wool/silk yarn (98yd/90m per ball) in dark purple
• **B** 1 x ⅞oz (25g) ball of fine-weight (4ply) metallic yarn (104yd/95m per ball) in gold
• **C** 1 x ⅞oz (25g) ball of fine-weight (4ply) metallic yarn (104yd/95m per ball) in purple

needles and notions

• 1 pair of size 9 (5.5mm) needles
• 1 size B1 (2.5mm) crochet hook
• Approx 500 gold and 200 wine 1in (24mm) flat sequins or paillettes with large hole at top

size

24in (61cm) wide and 36in (91.5cm) long (excluding fringe)

gauge

18 sts and 26 rows to 4in (10cm) measured over st st (1 row k, 1 row p) using size 9 (5.5mm) needles and yarn A

SPECIAL ABBREVIATIONS

PB Place sequin by inserting crochet hook through hole in sequin, hook next st off the left-hand needle and through the sequin. Place the st onto the right-hand needle without working it

knit note

The hole in the sequins (paillettes) should be big enough for two strands of yarn to go through. Make a bigger hole if necessary using a hole punch

> *TIP*
> For a lighter touch, choose transparent sequins with a hint of lilac or rose and set them against pale mint-green silk.

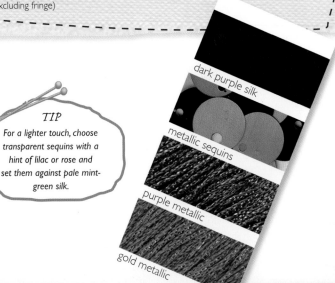

dark purple silk

metallic sequins

purple metallic

gold metallic

Knit your throw

Using size 9 (5.5mm) needles and A, cast on 109 sts.

Lower border

Work 6 rows in st st, starting with a k row.
Bead Row 1 K3, PB, (k5, PB) 17 times, k3.
Work 5 rows in st st.
**Bead Row 2 K6, PB, (k5, PB) 16 times, k6.
Work 5 rows in st st.
Bead Row 3 K3, PB, (k5, PB) 17 times, k3.
Work 5 rows in st st.**
Rep from ** to ** once more.
Work 5 rows in st st.

Side borders and centre panel

Bead Row 6 K6, PB, (k5, PB) twice, k71, PB, (k5, PB) twice, k6.
Work 5 rows in st st.

***Bead Row 7 K3, PB, (k5, PB) 3 times, k65, PB, (k3, PB) 3 times, k3.
Work 5 rows in st st.
Bead Row 8 K6, PB, (k5, PB) twice, k71, PB, (k5, PB) twice, k6.
Work 5 rows in st st.***
Rep from *** to *** until throw measures approx 31in (79cm) from beg.

Top border

Work Bead Row 1 once more.
Work 5 rows in st st.
Rep from ** to ** twice.
Bind off.

Making up

Sew in all ends neatly.

Each sequin (paillette) is hooked into place with a crochet hook. This is quite a slow process, but creates a stunning effect.

Fringe

Using A, wrap the yarn loosely several times around cardboard 12in (30cm) wide . Cut the wrapped strands at the bottom and remove the cardboard. Repeat for yarns B and C. Take two lengths of A and one length of B and fold in half. Using a crochet hook, pull the strands through the edge of the throw at one corner from front to back by catching the fold with the hook. Pass the ends through the folded loop and pull to tighten the knot. Make another tassel 1in (2.5cm) away from the first, using two lengths of A and one length of C. Continue in this way around the throw, alternating B and C with two strands of A, making each tassel 1in (2.5cm) apart.

Starting at one corner, take three strands from the first tassel and three strands from the next tassel and tie together with an overhand knot approx 1in (2.5cm) from the edge of the throw. Continue around the throw. Decorate the fringe by tying one gold and one wine sequin onto each tassel, and use the crochet hook to pull the yarn through the holes.

The fringe is made from three yarns: the yarn used from the main body of the throw, a metallic purple yarn, and a metallic gold yarn.

A mixture of gold and wine-red sequins create glinting flashes of colour amid the long fringe.

Knit Two

Enhance a vibrant ribbon yarn with fun, funky plastic beads to make this kitschy cushion. Simply knitted in stockinette stitch, it is made in two square pieces that are sewn shut once the cushion pad has been inserted. This fun, bold cushion is decorated with rows of brightly coloured pony beads, which are knitted into the fabric as you work.

The plastic beads in chunky, kitschy moulded shapes make a fabulously vivid contrast when set against the lime-green knitted fabric.

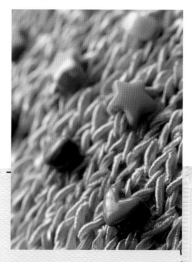

you will need

yarns
3 x 1¾oz (50g) balls of bulky-weight ribbon yarn (87yd/80m per ball) in bright lime green

needles and notions
• 1 pair of size 10 (6mm) needles
• 1 size B1 (2.5mm) crochet hook
• Pony beads in heart, star and barrel shapes – 8 of each shape in purple, yellow and pink
• 14in (35.5cm) cushion pad

size
14in (35.5cm) square

gauge
16 sts and 18 rows to 4in (10cm) measured over st st (1 row k, 1 row p) using size 10 (6mm) needles

SPECIAL ABBREVIATIONS
PB Place bead by inserting crochet hook through bead from top to bottom, hook next st off the left-hand needle and through the bead. Place the st onto the right-hand needle without working it

Knit your cushion

Front

Using size 10 (6mm) needles, cast on 57 sts.
Work 4in (10cm) in st st (1 row k, 1 row p).
**Bead Row 1 (Purple hearts) K14, PB, (k3, PB) 7 times, k to end.
Work 3 rows in st st.
Bead Row 2 (Pink stars) K16, PB, (k3, PB) 6 times, k to end.
Work 3 rows in st st.**
Rep from ** to ** 3 times more then rep Bead Row 1 once more, using beads in the following order: yellow barrels, purple stars, pink barrels, yellow hearts, purple barrels, pink hearts, yellow stars.
Work in st st until front measures 14in (35.5cm), ending with a p row.
Bind off.

Back

Using size 10 (6mm) needles, cast on 57 sts and work 14in (35.5cm) in st st, ending with a p row.
Bind off.

Making up

Sew in all ends neatly. Press according to instructions on ball band. Sew front to back around three edges. Insert cushion pad and sew remaining edge closed.

TIP

You could use pink heart-shaped beads on a pale pink fabric for a really feminine cushion, or bright yellow stars on silver for a space-age textile.

Abbreviations

Abbreviations are used in knitting patterns to shorten commonly used terms so that the instructions are easier to read and a manageable length. The following is a list of all the abbreviations you need to make the projects featured in your *How to Knit* box set and many of these are further explained later in this book. The green tinted box opposite lists the most common differences in US and UK knitting terms.

alt	alternate
approx	approximately
beg	beginning
C4B	cable 4 back
C4F	cable 4 front
Cr3L	cross 3 left
Cr3R	cross 3 right
cm	centimetre(s)
cont	continue
dec(s)	decrease/decreasing
DK	double knitting
dpn	double-pointed needles
foll	following
g	gram(s)
g st	garter stitch (k every row)
inc	increase(s)/increasing
in(s)	inch(es)
k	knit
k2tog	knit 2 stitches together (1 stitch decreased)
k3tog	knit 3 stitches together (2 stitches decreased)
k2togtbl	knit 2 stitches together through back of loops (1 stitch decreased)
kf&b	knit into front and back of stitch (increase 1 stitch)
m	metre(s)
mm	millimetres
M1	make one (increase 1 stitch)
oz	ounces
p	purl

US TERM	UK TERM
stockinette stitch	stocking stitch
reverse stockinette stitch	reverse stocking stitch
seed stitch	moss stitch
moss stitch	double moss stitch
bind off	cast off
gauge	tension

patt(s)	pattern(s)
PB	place bead
p2tog	purl 2 stitches together (1 stitch decreased)
p3tog	purl 3 stitches together (2 stitches decreased)
rem	remain/ing
rep(s)	repeat(s)
RS	right side
sk2po	slip 1 stitch, knit 2 stitches together, pass slipped stitch over (decrease 2 stitches)
sl	slip
sl2tog-k1-psso	slip 2 stitches together, knit 1 stitch, pass 2 slipped stitches over (2 stitches decreased)
ssk	slip 2 stitches one at a time, knit 2 slipped stitches together (1 stitch decreased)
st st	stockinette (stocking) stitch
st(s)	stitch(es)
tbl	through back of loop
tog	together
WS	wrong side
wyib	with yarn in back
wyif	with yarn in front
yd(s)	yards(s)
yo	yarn over
*	repeat directions following * as many times as indicated or end of row
[ ]	instructions in square brackets refer to larger sizes
( )	repeat instructions in round brackets the number of times

Yarn Details

Below are listed the specific yarns that were used for the projects in this book, should you wish to recreate them exactly. Yarn companies frequently discontinue colours or yarns, and replace them with new yarns. Therefore, you may find that some of the yarns or colours below are no longer available. However, by referring to the yarn descriptions on the project pages, you will have no trouble finding a substitute.

Substituting yarns

To work out how much replacement yarn you need follow these simple steps. Use it for each colour or yarn used in the project.

1 The number of balls of the recommended yarn x the number of yards/metres per ball = A

2 The number of yards/metres per ball of the replacement yarn = B

3 A ÷ B = number of balls of replacement yarn.

Ballerina Slipper Bling

Sirdar Bonus DK (100% acrylic – 306yd/280m per ball)
Main Project: 1 × 3½oz (100g) ball in 944 (Cupid)
Knit Two:
Embroidered slippers: 1 × 3½oz (100g) ball in 978 (Sunflower)

Button slippers: 1 × 3½oz (100g) ball in 998 (Turquoise)
Beaded slippers: 1 × 3½oz (100g) ball in 985 (Violet)

Knitted Trim Cushion
Main Project:
A 4 × 1¾oz (50g) balls of Kaalund Silk-stralis (50% silk/50% wool – 131yd/120m per ball) in Kikuyu
B 3 × 11yd (10m) skeins of Kaalund Silk Strands (100% silk) in each of Fuchsia, Nectarine and Magnolia
C 2 × 11yd (10m) skeins of Kaalund Silk Strands (100% silk) in Moss
Knit Two:
Feather trimmed: 5 × 1¾oz (50g) balls of Louisa Harding Kashmir Aran (55% merino/35% microfibre/10% cashmere – 83yd/75m per ball) in shade 06
Ribbon trimmed: 5 × 1¾oz (50g) balls of Rowan Classic Natural Silk Aran (73% viscose/15% silk/12% linen – 71yd/65m per ball) in shade 462

Pompom trimmed:
A 5 × 1¾oz (50g) balls of Rare Yarns
Cocoon (70% merino/15% alpaca/
7.5% silk/7.5% mohair – 110yd/100m
per ball) in Jade
1 × 1¾oz (50g) ball of Rare Yarns
Misty (50% alpaca/30% mohair/20%
merino – 110yd/100m per ball) in
Jade
1x 1¾oz (50g) ball of Rare Yarns
Astrakhan (80% alpaca/20% mohair
– 85yd/77m per ball) in Jade
1 × 1¾oz (50g) ball of Rare
Yarns Slub (30% suri alpaca/40%
tencel/20% acrylic/10% merino
– 73yd/67m per ball) in Fern

Intarsia Flower Bag
A 3 × 1¾oz (50g) balls of Rowan
Handknit Cotton DK (100% cotton
– 93yd/85m per ball) in colour 313
B 1 × 1¾oz (50g) ball of Rowan
Handknit Cotton DK (100% cotton
– 93yd/85m per ball) in colour 319
C 1 × 1¾oz (50g) ball of Rowan
Handknit Cotton DK (100% cotton
– 93yd/85m per ball)in colour 219

Sequinned Knitted Throw
Main Project:
A 10 × 1¾oz (50g) balls of Lang
Yarns Silkdream (50% merino/50%
silk – 98yd/90m per ball) in shade 80
B 1 × ⅞oz (25g) ball of Rowan Lurex
Shimmer (80% viscose/20% metal-
lized polyester – 104yd/95m per ball)
in shade 332
C 1 × ⅞oz (25g) ball of Rowan
Lurex Shimmer (80% viscose/20%
metallized polyester – 104yd/95m
per ball) in shade 338
Knit Two: 3 × 1¾oz (50g) balls of
Crystal Palace Yarns Party (100%
nylon – 87yd/80m per ball) in
shade 203

suppliers

Use the contact details listed below to help you to source the yarns and embellishments used for the projects in this book.

Crystal Palace Yarns
(US)
www.straw.com

(UK)
www.hantex.co.uk

Kaalund
(US)
email: donnaandaus@aol.com

(UK)
www.auscraft.co.uk

(AUS)
www.kaalundyarns.com.au

Lang Yarns
www.langyarns.ch

(USA)
www.berroco.com

(UK) Artyarn
www.artyarn.co.uk

Louisa Harding
www.louisaharding.co.uk

(USA)
www.knittingfever.com

(UK)
www.designeryarns.uk.com

Rare Yarns
www.rareyarns.com.au

Rowan
www.knitrowan.com

Rowan Classic Yarns
www.ryclassic.com

Sirdar
www.sirdar.co.uk

Other Books

For more about the following titles and other great knitting
books from David & Charles visit: **www.rucraft.co.uk**

*Knitter's Bible: Knitted
Throws & Cushions*

An inspiring selection of knitted projects to
brighten up your home, from luxury afghans and
bedspreads to functional cushions and seating.

Knitted Sock Sensations

Forget shoes; take your sock addiction to new
lengths with this fun and flirtatious collection of 40
knitted sock designs, with an inspiring mix
of cosy, quirky and chic.

Knitter's Bible: Knitted Bags

Featuring over 25 gorgeous knitted bags for
every occasion, from cool and casual to smart
and stylish. Uses many of the exciting yarns now
available for modern knitters.

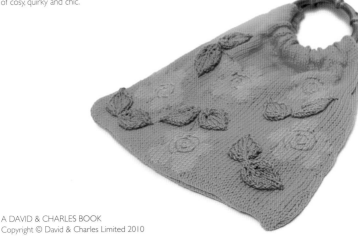

Contents

How To Knit:
Simple Knits

Introduction	2
GARTER STITCH SCARF	4
STOCKINETTE STRIP BAG	12
RIBBED TUBE SOCKS	20
SEED BAND BEDWARMER	30
Abbreviations	36
Yarn Details	38
Suppliers	40
Other Books	41

Introduction

Even though you are new to knitting, you will discover how you can create individual and exciting knitted projects in very little time without using complicated techniques. This book has some simple knitted projects to get you started.

There's the super-easy garter stitch scarf – all you need is some multi-coloured yarn and the basic knit stitch. Extending your skills to the knit and purl stitch (stockinette stitch) you can make a very useful bag – no shaping is involved here, just weaving together strips of knitted fabric. With a simple rib pattern, you can make your first pair of knitted socks, and why not try out your first textured stitch (seed [moss] stitch) by making yourself a cosy bedwarmer.

Not satisfied with bringing you four starter projects, extra ideas have been squeezed in for varying the patterns included, so look out for the Knit Twos or more. For the specific yarn details for all of the projects featured, see pages 38–39.

3

Garter stitch scarf

As a beginner to knitting, the first stitch you will learn is the knit stitch. When you knit each row, the fabric you make is called garter stitch. Garter stitch is great for knitting scarves because it looks the same from both sides and it lies nice and flat instead of curling in at the edges. This 'striped' scarf is made super-easy by using two balls of multi-coloured wool yarn of the same shade number. The yarn features long lengths of colour that are enough to knit two or three rows. Make sure to choose two balls that start with different colours to achieve the fantastic random stripe effect.

yarn
2 × 3½oz (100g) hanks of bulky weight (chunky) multi-coloured wool/silk mix yarn (131yd/120m per hank) in orange/green mix

needles and notions
• 1 pair of size 10½ (7mm) needles
• Size H/8 (5mm) crochet hook

size
5½in (13cm) wide by 64in (162cm) long (excluding tassels)

gauge
14 sts and 24 rows to 4in (10cm) measured over garter stitch (every row k) using size 10½ (7mm) needles

The tasselled fringe adds a pleasing embellishment to this scarf.

Knit your scarf
Label one ball A and the other ball B. Using size 10½ (7mm) needles and A, cast on 18 sts loosely and knit 2 rows.

Join in B and knit 2 rows.

Bring A in front of B and knit 2 rows with A.

Bring B in front of A and knit 2 rows with B.

Cont in garter stitch, working 2 rows in A then 2 rows in B, always bringing the new yarn in front of the old

at the beg of the row to keep the edge neat, until scarf measures 64in (162cm) long.
Bind off loosely.

Making up

To complete your scarf, all you need to do is to make the fringe. Wrap the yarn loosely around a piece of cardboard measuring 9in (23cm) wide. Cut the wrapped strands at the bottom and remove the cardboard. Take two lengths of yarn and fold in half. Using the crochet hook, pull the strands through the edge of the scarf from front to back by catching the fold with the hook. Pass the ends through the folded loop and pull to tighten the knot. Space each bunch of strands evenly along the edge.

Yarn change

You can use any yarn to knit a basic scarf. Just check on the ball band for the number of stitches to 4in (10cm). Decide on the finished width of the scarf and divide this measurement by 4in (10cm); for example, a 6in (15cm)-wide scarf would need one and a half times the stitch number, whereas a scarf 12in (30cm) wide would need three times the stitch number.

Garter stitch is such a simple fabric to produce that it is ideal for experimenting with yarns. You could use yarns of two different textures but in similar shades for the stripes – how about a mohair with a tweed

wool, or a crisp cotton with a soft chenille? Work two contrasting colours together; pink and green always fizzes with energy. Otherwise, try natural autumnal shades such as bronze and russet.

For a summer scarf use a soft medium-weight (aran) velour yarn and instead of a fringe, try adding an embellished button border. Here two sizes of shell buttons have been used.

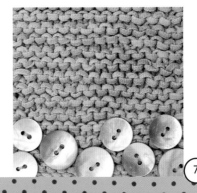

(7)

Knit Two

Here, garter stitch has been used to create a chic and colourful scarf from a drapey ribbon yarn. The light, slinky weight of the yarn and its fun, vibrant colours make it the perfect accessory to liven up a summer outfit. The appeal of this scarf lies both in its slinky, elegant drape and its fabulous rainbow colours. Even with a simple knitting technique, such as garter stitch, you can produce a dazzling many-coloured fabric using multi-dyed yarns.

you will need

yarn
4 × 1¾oz (50g) hanks of medium-weight (aran) viscose tape (68yd/62m per hank), multi-coloured

needles and notions
• 1 pair of size 10½ (7mm) needles
• Size H/8 (5mm) crochet hook

size
2¼in (5.5cm) wide by 92in (233cm) long

gauge
18 sts and 25 rows to 4in (10cm) measured over garter stitch (every row k) using size 10½/7mm needles

knit note
When using multi-coloured yarns, work with two balls at once. Knit two rows with ball A, then two rows with ball B. Knitting from one ball will produce blocks of colour, but using two balls will interrupt these colour blocks with a flash of another colour.

Knit your scarf

Label one ball A and the other ball B. Using size 10½ (7mm) needles and A, cast on 10 sts loosely and knit 2 rows.

Join in B and knit 2 rows.

Bring A in front of B and knit 2 rows with A.

Bring B in front of A and knit 2 rows with B.

Cont in garter stitch, working 2 rows in A then 2 rows in B, always bringing the new yarn in front of the old at the beg of the row to keep the edge neat, until scarf measures 92in (233cm) long.

Bind off loosely.

Making up

Sew in all ends neatly. Note that a knitted tape yarn will do what your knitting does if not bound off – it will unravel. To stop this happening, tie a small knot close to the end of each strand and cut the ends at an angle once you have woven them in. Use sewing thread to sew this into the fabric to make doubly sure. Make the fringe in the same way as for the garter stitch scarf using a piece of cardboard as wide as desired fringe and spacing each bunch of strands evenly along the edge. Knot the ends of the fringe to prevent them from unravelling.

The unique construction of knitted tape yarns lends this fabric its fabulous drape.

TIP

Garter-stitch scarves are great projects for beginners because you use only one stitch – you simply knit each row – and there is no shaping to worry about.

stockinette strip bag

This is a delightfully quirky bag that lets you run riot
with texture and details. The front of this patchwork
bag is made up of strips of stockinette stitch woven
together; each strip is worked in a different texture
or colour. The back is knitted in one piece in stripes.
After weaving the strips for the front, the pieces
are sewn together and secured further by adding
various buttons, charms and large beads. The handles
are knitted in garter stitch, and a single button and
loop provides the fastening. The finished size is a
very useful one for carrying large notepads and
folders around.

yarn

A 1 x 1¾oz (50g) ball of light-weight (DK) cotton/silk mix (218yd/200m per ball) in pale aqua
B 1 x ⅞oz (25g) ball of super-fine-weight (2ply) mohair yarn (229yd/210m per ball) in dark raspberry
C 1 x 1¾oz (50g) ball of light-weight (DK) cotton (115yd/106m per ball) in raspberry
D 1 x 1¾oz (50g) ball of medium-weight (aran) cotton/angora mix yarn (98yd/90m per ball) in aqua
E 2 x 1¾oz (50g) balls of light-weight (DK) alpaca/silk mix yarn (114yd/105m per ball) in raspberry

needles and notions

• 1 pair of size 7 (4.5mm) needles
• Button for fastening
• Selection of buttons, charms and large beads for embellishments
• Lining fabric 24½in (62cm) x 14¾in (37.5cm)
• Pencil, set square, ruler, paper (lining paper is ideal), pins and sewing thread

size

11in (28cm) wide and 13½in (34.5cm) long

gauge

18 sts and 24 rows to 4in (10cm) measured over st st (1 row k, 1 row p) using size 7 (4.5mm) needles and 2 strands of C

knit note

Yarns A, C and E use two strands together throughout. Use three strands of B together throughout. Make sure that you work through all strands for each stitch.

The yarn choice has been limited to just two colours, aqua and rich raspberry, which contrast well with each other. Once the colours have been chosen, try to collect together several yarns of different textures; for this project a dry cotton/silk mix, a crisp mercerized cotton, a luxurious mohair and an alpaca/silk mix have been selected and each texture shows the colours off differently.

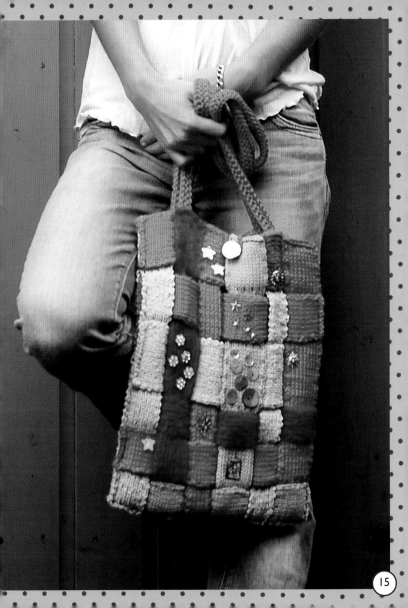

Knit your bag

Front
Vertical strips

Using size 7 (4.5mm) needles, yarn and number of cast-on sts as indicated, work 13½in (34.5cm) in st st (1 row k, 1 row p), starting with a k row and ending with a p row as follows:

Strip 1 Use 2 strands of A and cast on 8 sts.

Strip 2 Use 3 strands of B and cast on 10 sts.

Strip 3 Use 2 strands of C and cast on 6 sts.

Strip 4 Use 1 strand of D and cast on 12 sts.

Strip 5 Use 2 strands of A and cast on 6 sts.

Strip 6 Use 2 strands of C and cast on 10 sts.

Horizontal strips

Using size 7 (4.5mm) needles, yarn and number of cast-on sts as indicated, work 11in (28cm) in st st, starting with a k row and ending with a p row as follows:

Strip 1 Use 2 strands of E and cast on 12 sts.

Strip 2 Use 2 strands of C and cast on 10 sts.

Strip 3 Use 2 strands of A and cast on 14 sts.

Strip 4 Use 3 strands of B and cast on 8 sts.

Strip 5 Use 2 strands of E and cast on 10 sts.

Strip 6 Use 1 strand of D and cast on 10 sts.

Back

Using size 7 (4.5mm) needles and 2 strands of C, cast on 49 sts.
Using C, work 19 rows in st st, starting with a k row.
Using 2 strands of E, work 8 rows.
Using 2 strands of A, work 4 rows.
Using 3 strands of B, work 10 rows.
Using 1 strand of D, work 8 rows.
Rep this stripe sequence until back measures 12½in (32cm) from beg, ending with a p row.
Using 2 strands of C, knit 5 rows.
Bind off.

This project is an ideal way to use up yarn oddments. Try knitting each strip in a different colour for exciting contrasts.

Handles (make 2)
Using size 7 (4.5mm) needles and 2 strands of C, cast on 108 sts.
Knit 3 rows.
Bind off.

Making up
Sew in all ends neatly. Press according to the instructions on the ball bands, making sure the edges of the strips are lying flat.

Making a simple lining
Measure the length and width of the back. Draw a square or rectangle onto the paper using these measurements. Add a seam allowance of ⅝in (1.5cm) onto all sides. Cut out your paper pattern. Fold the lining fabric in half and pin the pattern on. Cut around the pattern, cutting through two thicknesses of fabric.

TIP
Adding a lining to your bag will make it stronger, more hard-wearing and will prevent the bag from stretching when full.

Match the lining to one of the yarn colours.

Weaving the front strips

On a flat surface, lay vertical strips in order next to each other. Weave the horizontal strips alternately under and over the verticals. Sew together around the outside edge, making sure the ends are level and corners are square. In some places where the strips cross over each other, sew a square of small running stitches to secure in a contrasting or matching yarn. Do this often enough so that the strips lay securely next to each and will not move. Sew on a selection of buttons and charms.

Assembling

Place back and front together with WS together. Sew around sides and base using a small running stitch. Sew fastening button in centre of front 1 in (2.5cm) below top edge. Using 2 strands of C, make a fastening loop in the centre of the back on the top edge. Begin by marking the position of the button loop on the back of the bag. Pin the button into place on the front. Thread a blunt needle with your yarn and secure it to the WS of the back just below the top edge to match the position of the button.

Vertical Strips

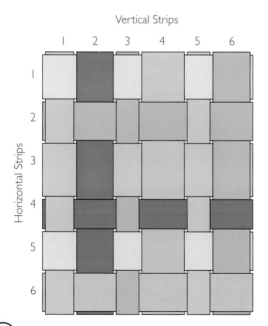

Horizontal Strips

Make a loop the required size by working loosely around the button placed on the front, then take the yarn to the back and secure. Take the needleback to the beginning again to make a double loop. Work buttonhole stitch (see *Basics*, page 34) over the loop, covering it from end to end. Work buttonhole stitch evenly around the loop. Sew on handles. With WS together, slip the lining into the bag and slipstitch neatly into place around the top of the bag, covering the ends of the handles.

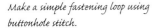

TIP
For the embellishments you could use pieces of broken jewellery or thrift-shop finds.

Make a simple fastening loop using buttonhole stitch.

The addition of the beads, buttons and charms makes the bag unique to you.

Ribbed tube socks

This project is perfect for the first-time sock knitter because there's no heel to turn. These funky tube socks have no shaping until the simple decreases for the toe. The support around the heel comes from the simple ribbed pattern that creates elasticity, hugging the contours of your foot. These socks are a great introduction to knitting in the round using double-pointed needles. As the name suggests, they are worked straight to form a tube, so you'll have plenty of time to get used to working with a handful of needles! To keep it simple to begin with, use just one colour, then when you get the hang of the technique, you can start adding colourful stripes.

yarn

2 × 1¾oz (50g) balls light-weight (DK) wool, acrylic and nylon mix yarn (131yd/120m per ball) in red

needles and notions

• 1 set of size 1 (2.5mm) double-pointed needles
• 1 set of size 4 (3.5mm) double-pointed needles
• Stitch marker

size

To fit three calf widths: Small [Medium: Large]. Overall length of sock is 20½in(53cm) but can be worked longer or shorter

gauge

Achieving an exact gauge is not essential for this project because the ribbing makes the knitted fabric stretchy

knit note

Read up on how to knit with double-pointed needles before you begin by turning to *Basics*, page 29.

Knit your socks (make 2)

Using size 1 (2.5mm) double-pointed needles, cast on 45 [51: 57] sts. Evenly distribute sts over 3 needles and place marker to indicate the beginning of the round.

Now work in the round, taking care not to twist sts.

Round 1 (k2, p1) to end of round.

Cont as set until knitting measures 1in (2.5cm).

Change to size 4 (3.5mm) double-pointed needles.

Cont in pattern until sock measures 19in (48cm).

TIP

Once you've got the hang of knitting in the round, you can start working some colour magic to make this simple pattern that much more fun to knit – and to wear.

There's no shaping at all in these tube socks until you decrease for the toe – instead, the stretchy ribbing will mould to the contours of your foot.

Shape toe

* Change to size 1 (2.5mm) double-pointed needles.
Work 3 rounds in pattern.
Next round (k2 tog, p1) to end of round.
Work 3 more rounds.
Next round K2tog to end of round.
K 1 round.

Making up

Transfer sts to 2 double-pointed needles and graft rem sts. Grafting is a way of sewing the toe stitches together in a way that imitates a knitted row of stitches. It creates a join that is invisible and seamless on both the right side and wrong side of the knitted fabric.

First divide the stitches equally between the 2 needles, one holding stitches for the top of the foot and the other holding stitches for the under part of the foot. Cut the yarn leaving about 30cm (12in) to graft the stitches with. Thread the yarn onto a darning needle. Insert the needle purlwise into the first stitch on the front needle and pull the yarn through. Insert the needle knitwise into the first stitch on the back needle and pull the yarn through.

Ensure that each needle ends on 2 knit stitches of the rib, so that ladders are not evident in the knitted fabric.

*Insert the needle knitwise into the first stitch on the front needle and slip the stitch off the needle. Insert the needle purlwise into the next stitch on the front needle and pull the yarn through. Insert the needle purlwise into the first stitch on the back needle and slip this stitch off the needle. Insert the needle knitwise into the next stitch on the back needle and pull the yarn through. Repeat from * to * until all the stitches have been grafted. Darn in any loose ends.

TIP

Just because your socks are long, doesn't mean you're short on looks. Turn them over, scrunch them down, or wear them high with pride.

Grafting creates a seamless and invisible join at the toe – see photograph opposite.

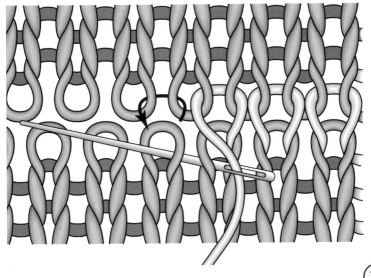

Knit Two

Now that you are comfortable working in the round, try adding some colourful stripes. Here thick stripes of contrasting lemon and lime are worked for a fresh, summery look.

you will need

yarn
• 1 x 1¾oz (50g) ball light-weight (DK) wool, acrylic and nylon mix yarn (131yd/120m per ball) in green
• 1 x 1¾oz (50g) ball light-weight (DK) wool, acrylic and nylon mix yarn (131yd/120m per ball) in yellow

needles and notions
As main project

size and gauge
As main project

Knit your socks
Work the basic pattern, swapping yarn colours every 1½in (4cm).

Knit Three

You'll love knitting these tube socks so much, you'll want another pair. For the tutti frutti version work four wide bands of colour around the calf, and four narrower bands at the toe.

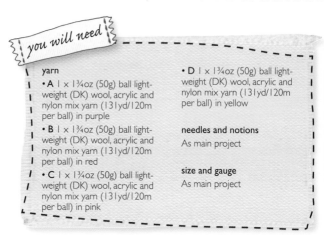

you will need

yarn

• **A** 1 × 1¾oz (50g) ball light-weight (DK) wool, acrylic and nylon mix yarn (131yd/120m per ball) in purple

• **B** 1 × 1¾oz (50g) ball light-weight (DK) wool, acrylic and nylon mix yarn (131yd/120m per ball) in red

• **C** 1 × 1¾oz (50g) ball light-weight (DK) wool, acrylic and nylon mix yarn (131yd/120m per ball) in pink

• **D** 1 × 1¾oz (50g) ball light-weight (DK) wool, acrylic and nylon mix yarn (131yd/120m per ball) in yellow

needles and notions
As main project

size and gauge
As main project

Knit your socks (make 2)

Cast on as for main project in yarn A. Work 1in (2.5cm) in rib patt. Change needle size.
Work 8 rounds in yarn B, 8 rounds in yarn C, 8 rounds in yarn D. Then change to yarn A and cont until work measures 17½in (44cm).
Work 4 rows in yarn B, 4 rows in yarn C, and 4 rows in yarn D.
Now change to yarn A and work toe as from *·

seed band bedwarmer

This small, sumptuously soft, heart-shaped bedwarmer is just the thing to snuggle into when you feel the cold. Alpaca has been used because of its warmth and beautiful softness, but as an alternative a soft, lush, wool yarn would also work well. This project is perfect for getting to grips with increasing and decreasing techniques, and the seed stitch band stripe across the front panel adds simple-to-knit texture. For a cosy, fragrant bed fellow, fill it with a cherry-stone bag and lavender sachets. The cherry-stone pad can be heated in the oven, and the heat of the cherry stones releases the soothing and relaxing aroma of the lavender.

yarn

2 x 1¾oz (50g) balls super-bulky-weight (super-chunky) alpaca or pure new wool

needles and notion

• 1 pair of size 15 (10mm) needles
• Stitch holder
• Darning needle
• Polyester or cotton wadding and sewing thread
• 10in x 16in (25cm x 40cm) of cotton fabric in a toning colour
• 2 large buttons about 1¼in (3cm) across
• Small lavender bag and small bag of cherry stones

size

Different yarns will knit up different sized bedwarmers: a super-chunky yarn will knit up one about 10in (25cm) across, while a more refined bulky yarn will produce an item around 8in (20cm) across.

gauge

Maintaining gauge is not essential for this project; just keep your stitches even and you should be fine

knit note

The heart is knitted up in three pieces. The front heart-shaped piece is knitted in stockinette stitch with a band of seed stitch across the middle. The back is knitted in two pieces, top and bottom, which are fastened together with two buttons. Yarnovers (yo) are used to create the buttonholes.

Alpaca fibre can be spun finely to give a cashmere-soft yarn, or left as thicker, unspun, strands to give a more fleecy effect as here.

Knit your bedwarmer

Back (bottom piece)
Using size 15 (10mm) needles, cast on 3 sts.

Row 1 Purl.

Row 2 (RS) Inc 1, knit to end, inc 1. 5 sts.

Cont in st st, increasing 2 sts as set every RS row until 25 sts.

Row 23 (WS) (k1, p1) to last stitch, k1. 25 sts.

Rep last row to set up seed stitch pattern.

Row 25 (k1, p1) 3 times, k2tog, (k1, p1) 4 times, k1, k2tog (p1, k1) 3 times. 23 sts.

Row 26 (Buttonhole row) (k1, p1) 3 times, k1, yo, (k1, p1) 4 times, k1, yo, (k1, p1) 3 times, k1. 25 sts.

Work 1 row, then bind off keeping seed stitch pattern intact.

Back (top piece)
Using size 15 (10mm) needles, cast on 25 sts and work 2 rows in st st, beginning with a knit row.

Row 3 K2togtbl, knit to last 2 sts, k2tog. 23 sts.

Row 4 Purl.

Row 5 K2togtbl, knit to last 2 sts, k2tog. 21 sts.

Row 6 P9, p2tog, p10. 20 sts.

Row 7 K2togtbl, k8, turn and work on these 9 sts only, putting remaining stitches on a stitch holder.

Row 8 P2tog, p7. 8 sts.

Row 9 K2togtbl, k4, k2tog. 6 sts.

Row 10 P2tog, p4. 5 sts.

Row 11 K2togtbl, k3. 4 sts.

Row 12 Bind off remaining 4 sts.

With RS facing, rejoin yarn to the work and remaining 10 sts.

Row 1 K8, k2tog. 9 sts.

Row 2 P7, p2tog. 8 sts.

Row 3 K2togtbl, k4, k2tog. 6 sts.

Row 4 P4, p2tog. 5 sts.

Row 5 K3, k2tog. 4 sts.

Row 6 Bind off remaining 4 sts.

Front
Using size 15 (10mm) needles, cast on 3 sts.

Row 1 Purl.

Row 2 (RS) Inc 1, k3, inc 1. 5 sts.

Row 3 Purl.

Cont in st st, increasing by 2 sts as set every RS row until 25 sts.

Row 23 (WS) (k1, p1) to last stitch, k1.

Work 4 further rows in seed stitch pattern.

Row 28 K2togtbl, knit to end, k2tog. 23 sts.

Row 29 Purl.

Row 30 K2togtbl, knit to end, k2tog. 21 sts.

Row 31 P9, p2tog, p10. 20 sts.

Row 32 K2togtbl, k8, turn and work on these 9 sts only, putting remaining stitches on a stitch holder.

Row 33 P2tog, p7. 8 sts.

Row 34 K2togtbl, k4, k2tog. 6 sts.

Row 35 P2tog, p4. 5 sts.

Row 36 K2togtbl, k3. 4 sts.

Row 37 Bind off remaining 4 sts.

With RS facing, rejoin yarn to the work and remaining 10 sts.

Row 1 K8, k2tog. 9 sts.
Row 2 P7, p2tog. 8 sts.
Row 3 K2togtbl, k4, k2tog. 6 sts.
Row 4 P4, p2tog. 5 sts.
Row 5 K3, k2tog. 4 sts.
Row 6 Bind off remaining 4 sts.

Making up

Darn in any loose ends. Pin out the knitting, right-side down, on to a padded surface or blocking board to form the correct heart shape. Cover with a damp cloth and press the wrong side gently with a hot iron. Leave to dry completely. Lay the front heart piece right-side down. Lay the top heart piece of the back on top, then position the bottom heart piece on top, with an overlay where the pieces meet. Mark where the buttonholes are, then sew on the buttons. Now sew the front to the back, sewing in the overlap of the button band.

Take the lining cotton and cut a piece as long as the opening on the back of the heart, and 10in (25cm) deep. Fold ¼in (1cm) over on each of the long ends and slipstitch ends into place. With right side in, fold the fabric in with hemmed edges, leaving a 1¼in (3cm) gap in the middle. Now stitch across the corners and snip off any excess fabric. Stitch the short ends into place, creating a long, thin envelope shape.

Stuff the heart with soft padding; you can vary the amount of padding or stuffing depending on whether you want a relatively squashy bedwarmer or a firmer, more resilient one. Slip the cotton envelope into place. Take the piece of cotton and slipstitch it into place, ensuring the cotton envelope does not obstruct the buttonholes. You may need to slipstitch the edges of the button flap together to hide any untidiness at the sides. Place a cherry-stone pad and a lavender bag into the pocket and button up.

TIP

The cherry-stone bag keeps its heat longer than a traditional hot-water bottle. Heat it in an oven at a maximum 150 degrees or in a microwave oven up to 600W for two minutes

Choose appropriately sized buttons that tone in attractively with the yarn.

Knit Two

This pattern can be used to make a pretty heart cushion. Make two front pieces and stitch together adding padding as you go.

Abbreviations

Abbreviations are used in knitting patterns to shorten commonly used terms so that the instructions are easier to read and a manageable length. The following is a list of all the abbreviations you need to make the projects featured in your *How to Knit* box set and many of these are further explained later in this book. The green tinted box opposite lists the most common differences in US and UK knitting terms.

alt	alternate
approx	approximately
beg	beginning
C4B	cable 4 back
C4F	cable 4 front
Cr3L	cross 3 left
Cr3R	cross 3 right
cm	centimetre(s)
cont	continue
dec(s)	decrease/decreasing
DK	double knitting
dpn	double-pointed needles
foll	following
g	gram(s)
g st	garter stitch (k every row)
inc	increase(s)/increasing
in(s)	inch(es)
k	knit
k2tog	knit 2 stitches together (1 stitch decreased)
k3tog	knit 3 stitches together (2 stitches decreased)
k2togtbl	knit 2 stitches together through back of loops (1 stitch decreased)
kf&b	knit into front and back of stitch (increase 1 stitch)
m	metre(s)
mm	millimetres
M1	make one (increase 1 stitch)
oz	ounces
p	purl

US TERM	UK TERM
stockinette stitch	stocking stitch
reverse stockinette stitch	reverse stocking stitch
seed stitch	moss stitch
moss stitch	double moss stitch
bind off	cast off
gauge	tension

patt(s)	pattern(s)
PB	place bead
p2tog	purl 2 stitches together (1 stitch decreased)
p3tog	purl 3 stitches together (2 stitches decreased)
rem	remain/ing
rep(s)	repeat(s)
RS	right side
sk2po	slip 1 stitch, knit 2 stitches together, pass slipped stitch over (decrease 2 stitches)
sl	slip
sl2tog-k1-psso	slip 2 stitches together, knit 1 stitch, pass 2 slipped stitches over (2 stitches decreased)
ssk	slip 2 stitches one at a time, knit 2 slipped stitches together (1 stitch decreased)
st st	stockinette (stocking) stitch
st(s)	stitch(es)
tbl	through back of loop
tog	together
WS	wrong side
wyib	with yarn in back
wyif	with yarn in front
yd(s)	yards(s)
yo	yarn over
*	repeat directions following * as many times as indicated or end of row
[ ]	instructions in square brackets refer to larger sizes
( )	repeat instructions in round brackets the number of times

Yarn Details

Below are listed the specific yarns that were used for the projects in this book, should you wish to recreate them exactly. Yarn companies frequently discontinue colours or yarns, and replace them with new yarns. Therefore, you may find that some of the yarns or colours below are no longer available. However, by referring to the yarn descriptions on the project pages, you will have no trouble finding a substitute.

Substituting yarns

To work out how much replacement yarn you need follow these simple steps. Use it for each colour or yarn used in the project.

1 The number of balls of the recommended yarn x the number of yards/metres per ball = A

2 The number of yards/metres per ball of the replacement yarn = B

3 A ÷ B = number of balls of replacement yarn.

Garter stitch scarf

Main Project: 2 x 3½oz (100g) balls of Noro Iro (75% wool/25% silk – 131yd/120m per ball) in colour 26
Swatch: GGH Velour (100% nylon – 63yd/58m per ball) in colour 13
Knit Two: 4 x 1¾oz (50g) hanks of Colinette Mercury (100% viscose – 68yd/62m per hank) in colour 146 Popsicle

Stockinette strip bag

A 1 x 1¾oz (50g) ball of Jaeger Trinity DK (40% silk/35% cotton/25% polyamide –218yd/200m per ball) in colour 432
B 1 x ⅞oz (25g) ball of Rowan Kidsilk Haze (70% kid mohair/30% silk – 229yd/210m per ball) in colour 606
C 1 x 1¾oz (50g) ball of Jaeger Aqua cotton (100% cotton – 115yd/106m per ball) in colour 322
D 1 x 1¾oz (50g) ball of Debbie Bliss cotton angora (80% cotton/20% angora – 98yd/90m per ball) in colour 15509
E 2 x 1¾oz (50g) balls of Debbie Bliss alpaca silk DK (80% alpaca/20% silk –114yd/105m per ball) in colour 26006

Ribbed tube socks

All projects use Patons Diploma Gold DK (55% wool, 25% acrylic, 20% nylon – 131yd/120m per ball)
Main Project: 2 x 1¾oz (50g) ball of 06129 (Berry)
Knit Two:
1 x 1¾oz (50g) ball of 06125 (Apple Green)
1 x 1¾oz (50g) ball of 06222 (Lemon)
Knit Three:
A 1 x 1¾oz (50g) ball of 06240 (Lupin)
B 1 x 1¾oz (50g) ball of 06129 (Berry)
C 1 x 1¾oz (50g) ball of 06158 (Hollyhock)
D 1 x 1¾oz (50g) ball of 06222 (Lemon)

Seed band bedwarmer

Main Project: 2 x 1¾oz (50g) balls of Karabella Brushed Alpaca (100% alpaca – 35yd/32m per ball) in shade 1074 (Lavender).
Knit Two: 2 x 1¾oz (50g) balls of Lana Grossa Caldo (100% wool – 38yd/35m per ball) in shade 64.

suppliers

Use the contact details listed below to help you to source the yarns and embellishments used for the projects in this book.

Colinette
(USA)
www.uniquekolours.com

(UK)
www.colinette.co.uk

Debbie Bliss
www.debbieblissonline.com

(USA)
www.knittingfever.com

(UK)
www.designeryarns.uk.com

(AUS)
www.prestigeyarns.com

GGH
www.ggh-garn.de

(USA)
www.muenchyarns.com

(UK)
www.getknitted.com

Jaeger
(USA)
e-mail: jaeger@westminsterfibers.com

(UK)
e-mail: mail@knitrowan.com

(AUS)
e-mail: sales@auspinners.com.au

Karabella
www.karabellayarns.com

Lana Grosso
www.lanagrossa.com

Noro
(USA)
www.knittingfever.com

(UK)
www.designeryarns.uk.com

(AUS)
www.prestigeyarns.com

Patons
(USA)
www.patonsyarns.com

(UK)
www.coatscrafts.co.uk

(AUS)
www.patons.biz

Rowan
www.knitrowan.com

Other Books

For more about the following titles and other great knitting
books from David & Charles visit: **www.rucraft.co.uk**

Knitter's Bible: Knitted Accessories

A collection of over 30 stylish knitted accessories
for all seasons, from gloves and scarfs, to hats and
ponchos. Easy-to-follow techniques
ensure great results for every project.

Knitter's Bible: Knitted Bags

Featuring over 25 gorgeous knitted bags for every
occasion, from cool and casual to smart and stylish.
Uses many of the exciting yarns now available for
modern knitters.

Two Balls or Less

Discover how a little yarn can go a long way with
20 irresistible quick-to-stitch knitting and crochet
projects, each requiring only two balls of yarn, or
less, to complete.

Knitted Sock Sensations

Forget shoes; take your sock addiction to new
lengths with this fun and flirtatious collection of 40
knitted sock designs, with an inspiring mix of cosy,
quirky and chic.